SHIPWRECKS OF CAPE COD

SHIPWRECKS OF CAPE COD

Stories of Tragedy and Triumph

Don Wilding

The History Press

Published by The History Press
Charleston, SC
www.historypress.com

First published 2021

Manufactured in the United States

ISBN 9781467147194

Library of Congress Control Number: 2021931123

In memory of

Noel Beyle
1941–2017

Jim Owens
1928–2018

Terri Rae Smith
1952–2019

Contents

Acknowledgements

This book would not have been possible without the help of a wide variety of friends on and off Cape Cod: historian Bill Burke at the Cape Cod National Seashore; the archivists at the Eastham Historical Society's 1869 Schoolhouse Museum; the Orleans Historical Society; the Pilgrim Monument and Provincetown Museum; Bob Seay, Shirley Weber, Debbie Abbott, Deborah Ullman and everyone at the Nauset Fellowship (U.U.) and Chapel in the Pines of Eastham; Phil and Charlotte Ryder; Richard Ryder; Phil Cole; Mary McDermott; M.J. Stevenson; Christopher Seufert; Jim Bickford; Cape Cod Coast Guard historian Richard Boonisar; Michael Lach and the Harwich Conservation Trust; Gene Guill and *Tales of Cape Cod*; Dave Drabkin; Pam Feltus; Tim Gerolami at the Wilkens Library of Cape Cod Community College; the staff at Sturgis Library in Barnstable; Paula Perrone at Highland Light in Truro; Jon March; Glenn and Sheila Mott; Tim Sweeney; and Robby "the Dune Tramp" McQueeney.

I'd also like to extend thanks to the dozens of organizations on Cape Cod and across New England that have hosted my Cape Cod history lectures since 2001.

Along with Noel Beyle, Jim Owens and Terri Rae Smith, there were many friends, no longer with us, who over the years contributed to this book becoming a reality, especially George Abbott and Nan Turner Waldron.

Many of the subjects chronicled in this book had their origins in my "Shore Lore" column for the *Cape Codder* newspaper in Orleans. Much gratitude goes out to Donna Tunney at the "Coddah."

Finally, I could never have accomplished any of this without the love and support of my mother, Harriet Wilding; my son, Matt Wilding; and my wife, Nita Wilding. Much love to you all.

Introduction

Cape Cod's Outer Beach has always been known for its shipwrecks. Between 1626 and the mid-twentieth century, this solitary forty-mile stretch of beach and sandbars saw the demise of more than three thousand vessels. It's been said that if all the wrecks were raised, one could walk from Provincetown to Chatham without getting his or her feet wet.

When Donald MacMillan was a boy growing up in nineteenth-century Provincetown, shipwrecks were a regular occurrence along the shores of the Outer Cape. The abundance of disasters forced the government to set up the U.S. Life-Saving Service in an effort to stop the loss of life. MacMillan later became known for his explorations of the Arctic region and achieved the rank of rear admiral and became so revered in Provincetown that the harbor pier was named in his honor. In 1965, McMillan recalled:

> *The thrilling cry of "Wreck ashore on the backside!" was often heard at school recess, and even whispered across the aisle. Impatiently we awaited the closing to the school session. Was it a ship or bark or brig from a foreign port, loaded with a rich cargo? Or was it one of the many fishing schooners running home from George's Bank? Such were very common, bound in from the fishing ground southeast of Highland. Many succeeded in finding the Cape and were lost endeavoring to find shelter in the harbor of Provincetown.*

Above: Many a ship met its end along Highland Light in Truro, which was the first lighthouse built on Cape Cod in 1797. *Sturgis Library Archives.*

Opposite: More than three thousand ships met their end along Cape Cod's outer beach. The wreck remains often drew not only curious residents but also wreckers in search of salvageable cargo. *M.J. Stevenson.*

In his book *Cape Cod*, Henry David Thoreau's encounter with the Cape begins with a shipwreck along the South Shore of Massachusetts:

> *We found that the Provincetown steamer, which should have got in the day before, had not yet arrived, on account of a violent storm; and, as we noticed in the streets a handbill headed, "Death! 145 lives lost at Cohasset!" We decided to go by way of Cohasset.*

According to the Thoreau Society, "The shipwreck becomes a symbol of a fragile, eggshell-like barrier between life and death. Thoreau is thus forced to consider this violent dichotomy on the shoreline, grappling to understand the dynamics of the sea and the shore as a kind of existential threshold."

Stories abound of wrecks along the Cape's eastern shores prior to the arrival of the *Mayflower* in 1620. Portuguese fishermen and explorers are thought to have landed here before the voyages of Columbus. In 1616, a French ship wrecked along the Cape's outer shore, and the handful of survivors were captured and tortured by the Nausets. The *Mayflower* nearly became a statistic itself, as the ship, bound for Virginia, drifted farther north than planned. The land now known as Eastham was first spotted by the Pilgrims, who turned south but nearly ran aground along the shoals

of Monomoy before turning north for what Captain John Smith named "Milford Haven," which is now known as Provincetown Harbor.

The *Sparrow-Hawk* was the first of the wrecks along this treacherous coast, and the numbers didn't decrease until nearly 350 years later, following technological improvements and the establishment of the Cape Cod Canal, first built in 1914 and then widened during the 1930s.

As Europeans continued to settle along the coast, the rate of wrecks increased, particularly during the winter months. This led to the founding of the Massachusetts Humane Society by a group of Boston citizens in 1786. Lifesaving equipment, lifeboats and shelters were established on the islands and coastal areas of Massachusetts, and volunteers were enlisted to assist in rescue missions.

McMillan noted, "Benjamin Franklin was the first to recognize the dangers inherent in the troubled waters of Cape Cod and through his efforts, a strong light was established at Highland" in 1797. More lighthouses followed—two beacons at Chatham in 1817, Race Point in Provincetown and the "Three Sisters" of Nauset in Eastham in 1837.

Sadly, these efforts wouldn't be enough. In 1872, the U.S. Life-Saving Service took shape, and nine stations (later expanded to thirteen) were set up between Long Point in Provincetown and Monomoy Island, south of Chatham. The Life-Saving Service was later merged with other government agencies into the U.S. Coast Guard in 1915. Thousands of lives were saved by the brave efforts of these men. Many shipwreck remains were covered quickly by the Cape's shifting sands, while others remained on the shore for decades or even centuries. Wreckers salvaged whatever cargo they could before the elements took over, while the shattered timbers of wrecks became shoreline exhibits for local residents.

In this book, we'll look at a small sample of these wrecks and rescues. Many Cape Cod shipwreck stories—such as the *Whydah* (1717), the *Pendleton* (1952) and the "Portland Gale" (1898)—have been told elsewhere. We'll uncover some of the tales of triumph and tragedy that have been unveiled as much as a shipwreck's skeleton in the sand. As Isaac M. Small wrote in 1912:

> *Out there today when the tide is low, protruding through the sands of the bar and the white caps that wash them, are the broken fragments of the sunken ship looking like tombstones in the village churchyard. All along the shores of this windswept and sea washed coast these half-submerged and silent sentinels remind us that up and down this sandy reach the ever moving sea has covered hundreds of those heroic men who have gone down in ships on the great sea.*

SPARROW-HAWK

CAPE COD'S FIRST SHIPWRECK

In December 1626, the *Sparrow-Hawk* was en route from Portsmouth, England, to Jamestown, Virginia, when the overloaded and off-course vessel stranded on a flat in an area that was known as Monomoyick. The captain was ill with scurvy, and the water and wood supplies were nearly gone. Upon running aground, the crew had no idea where they were.

The *Sparrow-Hawk* washed ashore off the Pochet Island area of Nauset Beach in Orleans on December 17, 1626, with forty immigrants and crew members. Although other ships are believed to have stranded along these shores before, the *Sparrow-Hawk* is generally classified as the first wreck on Cape Cod shores.

Landfall was made the next day—abeam of a small blind harbor before which they anchored. "Readying a boat to go ashore, then a sudden gale accompanied by heavy seas came on during which the ketch broke away from the anchor and drove over the bar, sweeping the ship into the harbor and on to the flats," wrote Orleans historian Al Snow in the April 9, 1950 edition of the *Cape Codder*.

Natives were seen paddling across the bay toward them in two canoes. Fearing an attack, firearms were broken out and loaded as the men waited under the hull. One native came up and spoke in English, asking if they were friends of the governor of Plymouth; he informed the *Sparrow-Hawk* crew where they were. The natives bargained to take a message to Governor William Bradford in Plymouth, and the English gave them some trinkets and colored cloths in exchange for food.

Bradford received the message and prepared a boat with supplies for a trip across Cape Cod Bay to Namskaket Creek. From there, the natives helped to move the supplies via trails to Arey's Pond and then canoed over to Portanumicut Harbor. These supplies included corn, pumpkins and tools needed to repair the ship. The *Sparrow-Hawk*'s planking was fastened with iron spikes and caulked. Repairs were finished several days later, and natives helped move the vessel back into the harbor.

Another storm hit, stranding the vessel in nearly the same spot as before. Another message was sent to Plymouth alerting Bradford of the new problems and a request to stay at Plymouth until another ship could take them to Virginia. The *Sparrow-Hawk* passengers were allotted land in Plymouth, and they stayed until June 1627, when a ship heading for Virginia picked them up.

John Sibsey was one of the leaders of the *Sparrow-Hawk* group. Although Sibsey found himself living with Pilgrims at Plymouth following the *Sparrow-Hawk* disaster, he didn't have a lot in common with them. Prior to the wreck, Sibsey originally settled in northern part of Virginia, near the James River, and was in the process of going back and forth to England to get servants. He later became a "burgess" (a governor of sorts) after returning to Virginia in 1627.

"The character himself is not a Separatist," according to actor David Hobbs, who has portrayed Sibsey in Massachusetts. "He's not sympathetic to their church. He just wants to get out of there and get back to his plantation in Virginia, which he opened in 1617. He wasn't particularly fond of the King's Church, but he knew which side his bread was buttered on, so he was a member."

The *Sparrow-Hawk*'s remains were eventually buried by a storm and would not reemerge until 237 years later. On May 6, 1863, following a two-day storm, the *Sparrow-Hawk*'s oak hull was discovered by two East Orleans beachcombers, Solomon Linnell and Alfred Rogers.

Linnell and Rogers were "walking south beside their ox-team," searching for driftwood, according to a May 5, 1963 article by Al Snow in the *Cape Cod Standard-Times*. They realized it was an ancient hull and "chose to wait a while before breaking her up to allow others a chance to examine" it.

Orleans residents came from town or crossed Pleasant Bay by boat to check it out. Many took pieces of it as souvenirs. "Some folks were positive it was a Viking hull," Snow noted, while others thought it might be the *Mary Anne*, a vessel seized by Captain Sam Bellamy of the *Whydah* in 1717.

A model of the British vessel *Sparrow-Hawk*, which was the first record of a shipwreck on Cape Cod. It ran aground along Nauset Beach in Orleans in December 1626. *Eastham Historical Society.*

It was reported that when the ship was uncovered, "the ship's upper works had been burned away by Indians in search of metals, cattle bones, pieces of shoe leather, and a metallic box," which were "found in the hull."

The *Sparrow-Hawk*'s timbers were visible from time to time until the Linnell-Rogers discovery. Word quickly got out to the likes of Jean Louis Agassiz, founder of the Marine Biological Laboratory at Woods Hole, and historian Amos Otis, who "took careful measurements, making accurate diagrams of the hull," according to Snow. Boston city councilor Charles Livermore pushed to bring the hull to Boston for exhibit. The frame also made its way to Providence for an exhibit, "with the end result a financial fiasco to the promoters," Snow noted.

According to an undated newspaper story from the Eastham Historical Society archives, Almenia Brewer of Eastham came to possess a hand-carved cane from the *Sparrow-Hawk*'s timbers. Her father, Reuben Brewer, took home several pieces of the wreck as souvenirs. One of the relics was carved into a cane by Russell Doane of Eastham.

The cane was described as being "of well seasoned oak, rubbed and polished to a fine finish. The rounded head is pegged with wood both lighter and darker than the main body and the ferrule with diamond shaped inlays of similar wood. Two brass rings, now green with age, complete the decorations. It appears as sturdy as the day it was new."

HMS *Somerset*

Terror to the Coast

During the American Revolution, one of the great adversaries of the New England colonists was the fearsome presence of the British man-of-war HMS *Somerset*. But when the *Somerset* ran aground on the Peaked Hill Bars off Provincetown's back shore on November 2 and 3, 1778, a great sense of relief was felt across Cape Cod and the rest of the region.

Of the *Somerset*'s crew of 480, 21 perished in the stranding, while the survivors, including Captain George Aurey, were taken prisoner by the townspeople of Truro and Provincetown and marched to Boston.

The *Somerset*'s roles in the Battle of Bunker Hill, Paul Revere's ride and other Boston-area conflicts and events during the American Revolution are well documented. For the next few years, the *Somerset* remained "about Cape Cod and the adjacent shores, capturing and burning much of the American commerce, and being generally a terror to the unprotected coast," according to the 1886 article "The Wreck of the *Somerset*" by *Boston Post* editor and publisher E.A. Grozier:

> [The Somerset was often anchored in Provincetown Harbor, and its] *boats frequently landed, and the officers helped themselves to water, provisions, and anything else that they wanted. In return for the unwilling assistance thus given him, Captain Aurey sometimes sent the chaplain ashore to preach to the people and tell them how wicked and unchristian it was to cherish any rebellious feelings against King George.*

The presence of the *Somerset* was so frightening to the locals that parents used it to keep their children in line. Cape Cod mothers would tell their children that the black-whiskered pirate Captain George Aurey was coming after them in his big ship.

Despite the hostilities between the locals and the British soldiers, it didn't stop several romantic relationships from blossoming. The surgeon of one of the British ships was said to have been so infatuated with a young Truro woman that he left the service of the king and settled permanently on the Cape, where, as Grozier noted, "descendants bearing his name are living to this day."

On the fateful day, word had spread that the British frigate was in hot pursuit of a French vessel along the Cape's back shore, drawing a large crowd to High Pole Hill in Provincetown. With a storm moving in and the northeast gales increasing, "the *Somerset* found herself on a lee-shore, in more danger than she had ever been from the guns of her enemies," Grozier wrote. The crew began dropping its weapons overboard in the hopes of lightening its load, but the

The remains of the British warship HMS *Somerset* emerged from its sandy grave along Provincetown's Peaked Hill Bars in 1973. *Phil Ryder.*

disabled ship struck on the Peaked Hill Bars and had washed onto the beach the next morning by the high tide. When it did, the locals, who had crowded the beach, were waiting. As Grozier noted:

> *A detachment of militia marched down from Truro, took possession of the wreck and made prisoners of the captain and crew in the name of the Commonwealth. Colonel Doane of Wellfleet was put in charge of the frigate. The prisoners were marched to Barnstable and then Boston. Captain Aurey was fortunate enough to secure an exchange as prisoner of war.*

The remains of the wreck were eventually covered by the shifting sands. In 1886, the remains were exposed for the first time. One of the cannons and the cathead, which was an ornamental fitting in the bow used to secure the anchor, were among the items recovered. Timbers were also uncovered in 1973 and 2012, although they were quickly buried again by the sands.

However, nothing may match the jubilation felt by the people on High Pole Hill on that November day. "A shout went up from the watchers on the hill," Grozier wrote. "They knew they would suffer no more from the depredations of the *Somerset*."

Like the *Sparrow-Hawk*, the wreck of the *Somerset* also produced a cane. According to the *Yarmouth Register* of September 18, 1886:

> *Samuel Knowles, Esq., has presented W.H.H. Weston of Plymouth with a handsome cane made from a piece of the British frigate Somerset. The cane has sperm whale's tooth for a handle, and is a very neat article.*

The Truro Gale of 1841

Then shall the dust return to the
earth as it was and the spirit shall
return unto God who gave it.
Man goeth to his long home and the
mourners go about the street.
—monument inscription at the Truro Congregational Church cemetery

If anyone ever wondered what the darkest days in Truro's history were, just wander into the far western end of the Truro Congregational Church cemetery. That's where an obelisk stands, paying tribute to the fifty-seven town men who lost their lives at sea during the tragic "October Gale" that lashed New England during the first week of October 1841. Only a few of the bodies were recovered. "The loss in this storm was the most serious calamity that ever visited the town," wrote Sidney Perley in his 1891 book, *Historic Storms of New England.*

Eight of the victims were from the Snow family; eight others were Paines. Three boys under the age of thirteen, the youngest being eleven, also lost their lives. Their "homes were in a circuit of two miles—twenty-seven of them were married, and only eight over thirty years of age," wrote Boston publisher Maturin Murray Ballou in 1856. "The population at that time was about 1,900; the number of widows, 105."

The widows in town became reluctant to marry anyone who made his living at sea. When Henry David Thoreau passed through Truro during

This page: An obelisk pays tribute to the fifty-seven residents of Truro who were lost in the "October Gale of 1841." *Author's collection.*

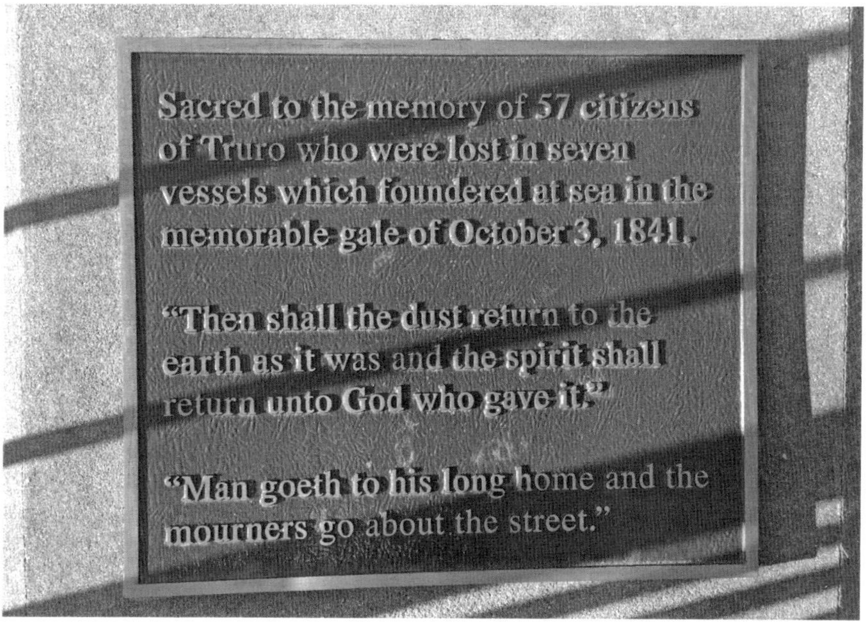

his trips, which would be chronicled in the book *Cape Cod*, he asked a Truro resident, "Who lives in that house?"

"Three widows," he was told.

Somehow, three members from two Truro vessels—the *Garnet* and the *Water Witch*—managed to survive.

The *Garnet*'s plight was documented by its captain, Joshua Knowles. After sailing out of Provincetown Harbor on October 2, the storm kicked in, eventually breaking up the vessel, but it held together enough for the crew to stay afloat. As the severe conditions abated, the crew members found some potatoes floating in the water and managed to cook their first meal in two days before the *Roscius*, a Liverpool packet captained by John Collins of Truro, saw their distress flag and plucked them out of the sea. The *Water Witch*, a schooner captained by Matthias Rich, managed to anchor itself safely in Herring Cove, just south of Hatches Harbor and Race Point.

Overall, the storm wrecked more than 190 vessels off the New England coast, with property losses totaling more than $2 million (more than $55 million today). Between the Truro Highlands and Chatham, more than forty vessels ran aground, and fifty bodies were found on the beach.

Other Cape towns were affected by the tragedy. Dennis lost twenty-six men, while ten from Yarmouth perished. Eighteen Harwich vessels were wrecked. "The ocean roared as though with an unbridled madness, and its waves ran mountain high, throwing their spray far into the sky, and forming a majestic yet fearful sight," Perley wrote.

Many more vessels from Truro were fishing off George's Bank, near Sable Island or near the Nantucket Shoals. The *Pomona*, captained by twenty-three-year-old Solomon Dyer, was found bottom-up in Nauset Harbor, with three boys drowned in the cabin. The *Dalmation*, with Captain Daniel Snow and a crew of ten, was lost. Among the other Truro ships claimed by the storm were the *Altair* (captained by Elisha Rich), the *Arrival* (captained by Freeman Atkins Jr.), the *Cincinnatus* (captained by John Wheeler) and Reuben Snow's vessel, the *General Harrison*.

Inland, at least a foot of snow fell from Connecticut up into Vermont and New Hampshire. That would quickly melt away, but the memory of the October Gale of 1841 endures on the Outer Cape to this day.

FRANKLIN

"WRECKED FOR PROFIT"

It was no worse than a good many other shipwrecks in Cape Cod history. But for two causes other than the sad toll of death the wreck of the Franklin *is of special interest.*
—*Donald Trayser,* Provincetown Advocate, *March 31, 1949*

Cape Cod's Outer Beach saw more than three thousand shipwrecks during the years between 1626 and the mid-twentieth century, but the horrors surrounding the wreck of the *Franklin* on March 3, 1849, off Wellfleet were particularly disturbing, in more ways than one. The *Provincetown Advocate* stated that "the *Franklin* is the only vessel known to have been deliberately wrecked on Cape Cod for profit."

The *Franklin* disaster was "one of the most appalling disasters that ever occurred on Cape Cod," J.W. Dalton wrote in his 1902 book, *The Lifesavers of Cape Cod*. "Speedy retribution came to the officers of the ship for their terrible crime, the captain and nearly all the others losing their own lives in the wreck."

According to the notes encased in a valise that was later recovered on the beach by thirteen-year-old Benjamin Rich, the "crime" was Captain Charles Smith conspiring with the ship's owners, James W. Wilson and John W. Crafts of Boston, to sink the vessel, heading for Boston from Deal, England, for the insurance money. Fifteen people died while attempting to row to shore in a lifeboat after the ship struck the sandbar. Wilson pled guilty in federal court but didn't serve any jail time after Crafts was found not guilty. As Donald Trayser wrote in the March 31, 1949 edition of the *Provincetown Advocate*:

> [Wilson] *confessed that he had conspired to cast away the ship, but his partner* [Crafts] *denied guilt and at the close of the longest trial in the history of Massachusetts, was acquitted. Evidence against the owners came to light in storybook fashion.*

The *Advocate* added that because of the moderate weather conditions, the *Franklin* should never have struck the beach.

Many people observed the disaster from shore, including the "Wellfleet Oysterman" from Henry David Thoreau's book *Cape Cod.* After being alerted about the wreck, the oysterman observed the locals preparing a boat on the beach, but rough surf prevented any kind of rescue. Aboard the ship, passengers were on deck, getting into the lifeboat, and the oysterman told his visitor from Concord:

> *"I saw the captain get out his boat. He had one little one; and then they jumped into it one after another, down as straight as an arrow. Then they shoved off." One swept over the boat, dumping three passengers into the sea. The next wave turned the boat bottom upward, and emptied them all out. None of them ever came ashore alive.*

Fortunately for the passengers left on the ship, which was breaking up, they were rescued by the boat from shore. However, a long trial awaited the ship's owners. Trayser wrote the following summary for the *Advocate*:

> *But after thirty days of hearing evidence which, it must be remarked, painted the confessing partner a pretty black villain, the jury was doubtful and acquitted* [Crafts], *although its verdict did not negate Wilson's confession, or the strong evidence of the deliberate wrecking of the* Franklin.

The *Franklin*'s cargo consisted of wood, nutmeg, books and dry goods, but a large quantity of the cargo belonged to South Boston's Robert J. Bell, who had been in England and Scotland picking out trees and shrubs for a horticultural establishment that he was to open in Boston. Bell invested his life savings in the project, and most of these washed ashore along the

In his book *Cape Cod*, writer Henry David Thoreau recalled the story of the *Franklin*, told to him by the "Wellfleet Oysterman." *Library of Congress.*

Cape's Outer Beach. "Into Wellfleet barns and homes it went, and soon, into Wellfleet soil. To this day there are trees, lindens, pear, apple, plum and other fruit trees; roses and lilies," Trayser wrote. Thoreau later saw many of the trees growing in a garden that originated from Bell's seedlings and shrubs.

According to the 1900 U.S. Life-Saving Service report, Benjamin Rich was a crew member working under his father's command. On one of the trips, the rescuers carried ashore an infant whose mother had perished, and young Rich held the child in his arms. The child was barely alive when they landed but survived many years to become "one of the first of the industrious and frugal matrons of the Cape." For heroism in saving twenty-one lives, both father and son were awarded medals of honor by the Humane Society.

Josephus

Hell at Highland Light

Why, men, you are crazy to do this, you cannot possibly reach that ship, and your lives will pay the forfeit of your foolhardy attempt.
—Isaac M. Small, Shipwrecks of Cape Cod, *1928*

During the late night hours of April 1, 1849, Highland Light keeper Enoch Hamilton was finishing up what had been a horrific day of events along Truro's Outer Beach. Twenty-five souls had perished during the wreck and attempted rescue of the British ship *Josephus* just north of the lighthouse, and Hamilton decided to check the beach one more time to see if any more bodies had washed ashore.

Hamilton found something all right, but not quite what he expected. "What was his surprise to find upon a piece of the cabin of the ship, which had washed ashore, a helpless sailor moaning piteously, still alive but suffering terribly from the hardships he had endured," wrote Truro historian Isaac M. Small in his 1928 book, *Shipwrecks of Cape Cod*. This was the first of many disasters witnessed by Small. He was all of four years old when this "full rigged ship" event occurred, and along with his mother, he watched the tragedy's aftermath unfold from the beach.

The *Josephus* was headed to Boston, carrying a load of iron, but fog and stormy weather sent it crashing into the sandbar a half mile from shore. The distressed vessel was spotted from the lighthouse, and it wasn't long before the locals were on the beach, wondering what could be done to rescue the twenty-four men on board.

Enter Daniel Cassidy and Jonathan Collins, two young men who had just returned from a fishing voyage. Ignoring the warnings from those on the beach, Cassidy and Collins attempted a daring rescue by way of a surfboat. Unfortunately for the duo, those concerns proved to be correct. Cassidy and Collins would get no farther than fifty yards out before they were overcome by the surf. By nightfall, "the cries of the sailors grew fainter and ceased," according to Small, and the locals soon gave up hope and went home for the night.

At midnight, Hamilton, who had been attending to the lighthouse lamps, made one more check on the beach and found the survivor. Somehow, Hamilton managed to drag the man along the beach, up the massive sandy cliff and into the lighthouse before summoning a local doctor.

Amazingly enough, the sole survivor of the *Josephus* tragedy recovered. As Small noted, "He was the only man of that ship's company of twenty-four souls who escaped with life, these and the two men who attempted a rescue made a total death list in this disaster of twenty-five."

CLARENDON

"ONE OF 'EM WAS DEAD"

That dead man sat right up in the opening.
—Isaiah Young, as told to the Boston Globe, *1904*

The Outer Beach of Cape Cod certainly saw its share of shipwrecks throughout its history, and with it came its share of people who perished before they could be rescued. The job of being a rescuer for the Massachusetts Humane Society, the U.S. Life-Saving Service and the U.S. Coast Guard could be traumatic in so many ways, especially when it involved retrieving the bodies of those who died. Now imagine their surprise when one of those victims, presumed dead, turned out to be alive.

That's what happened during the wreck of the schooner *Clarendon* on the back shore of Provincetown during a storm on January 5, 1856, when the quintet of Humane Society volunteers Isaiah Young, Isaac F. Mayo, Amos Chapman, Otis Lovering and Richard Chapman boarded a surfboat to rescue the distressed vessel four hundred yards offshore. On a fourth attempt, they maneuvered through a maelstrom sea to rescue the crew of five men, who had climbed into the masts to avoid the towering waves crashing over the inner bar.

"One of 'em was dead," Young, nineteen at the time of the *Clarendon* rescue, recalled for the *Boston Globe* in 1904. "That is, all hands thought so at the time, because he was hanging, stark and stiff, only kept from falling into the sea by a rope that bound him to the shrouds." While the other four

The body of a shipwreck victim is pulled ashore off a Cape Cod beach. In the case of the *Clarendon* wreck, one of those victims was still alive. *Sturgis Library Archives.*

men were taken to the surfboat, the "life car" was employed to move "the supposedly dead man," as Young put it:

> *When we left the shore we took along the end of a line that was coiled on the beach, thinking that the car might be needed, so, when we found one man had succumbed, we hauled back the car from the beach to the schooner by means of that rope and, working between seas, made out to balance it across the nearly submerged rail.*

The body was put into the car and it was cut loose, but it ended up being caught in a current, sending it a mile and half westward before the rescuers could recover it and then open it. As Young recalled:

> *Either the heat from the metal had drawn the frost out of him or the bumping he sustained while the little car was rolling over in the surf had brought him back to life.*

This was Young's first lifesaving feat. Each one of the rescuers was awarded one of the medals that the Massachusetts Human Society awarded to volunteers in those days. He joined the U.S. Life-Saving Service after it was formed in 1872 but was forced to give it up after sustaining injuries in the rescue of the *C.E. Trumbull* in 1880. For Mayo, he would lead another rescue attempt, in the same boat, twenty-four years later.

The *Clarendon* rescue remained fresh in Young's mind when the *Globe* finally caught up with him in 1904, when he was sixty-eight. "That's about all there is to that story," Young concluded. "Except to say that we went ashore with the rest of the sailors right side up, the boat being a good one."

Shipwrecked Swine in 1854

A wide variety of animals can be spotted on any given day along Cape Cod's Outer Beach. Pigs aren't usually one of them, but it happened along the North Truro shore on October 23, 1854, just prior to the demise of an unknown brig that was carrying the critter through stormy seas. "As she drove along the surf opposite Highland Station a great brown pig was swept from her deck and came rolling up in the surf on the shore," wrote Isaac M. Small in his 1928 book, *Shipwrecks on Cape Cod*. "He was a good swimmer and had made the stance, somewhat out of breath but intact."

According to the August 12, 1948 edition of the *Provincetown Advocate*, the pig "washed from a pen on deck, which managed to swim ashore near Highland Light." The seven members of the crew weren't as fortunate. They would later perish when their out-of-control vessel was swept across Massachusetts Bay and struck the rocks at Scituate.

Late in the afternoon, observers on the Cape cliffs noticed the erratic motion of the ship before it was carried north. "With a telescope, the lighthouse watchers could see mountainous seas pouring over the deck, forcing the crew of seven men to climb and lash themselves in the rigging," the *Advocate* noted.

According to Small, the men "were clinging desperately above the raging sea which was pouring in torrents across the vessel's deck, making any attempt to regain the use of the wheel impossible." The vessel was swept around Race Point into Massachusetts Bay, eventually crashing into the rocky shores of Scituate, located between Boston and Plymouth.

After waddling ashore from the rough surf, the pig ended up as a very fortunate Cape Cod washashore. The identity of the ship, however, remained a mystery. "A spectator took him home and he grew to be a big and lusty porker," Small wrote. "If he could have talked we would have known the name of his ship."

ORISSA

TRAGEDY AND A LIFELONG FRIENDSHIP

Her birth coincided with the wreck of the ship Orissa *near the Linnell home. Her parents were so impressed that she was named for the ship and given the name of the ship's captain as a middle name.*
—obituary of Orissa Sears Linnell, Yarmouth Register, *September 10, 1943*

The evening of January 19, 1857, was a truly eventful night in the East Orleans home of Captain Dean Gray Linnell, who was in charge of the two huts of the Massachusetts Humane Society, and Mehitable F. (Rogers) Linnell. The couple welcomed a new daughter into the world only hours after four men met their end in the tragic shipwreck of the *Orissa* on Nauset Beach.

Cyrus Sears, captain of the *Orissa,* was among the survivors taken to Linnell's home. It was here that a lifelong friendship was struck up between the longtime seaman and the young girl—an amazing feat, considering what the crew of the *Orissa* had just been through.

Late in 1896, the *Orissa* had left India on its way to Boston, carrying a load of "hides, gunny cloth, linseed, and ginger," as Sears described in an account for the *Cape Cod Item* and the *Chatham Monitor* on February 2, 1897. The *Orissa* passed around the Cape of Good Hope, and preparations were made for winter weather. They didn't have long to wait. By the time the *Orissa* reached the Gulf Stream, a gale had damaged the vessel's sails and cost it the quarter boat. On January 16, snow and sleet, driven by northeasterly gales, kicked in. Even though the conditions were worsening, the ship's position was favorable for entry into Boston Harbor. By Monday morning, trouble was brewing, as Sears recalled:

> *About 5 a.m. Monday morning the soundings had decreased to thirty-six fathoms. Then came the momentous question—were we drifting into Boston Bay, and were the soundings those of Stelwagen Bank, or were we on the back of Cape Cod?*

It was determined that they would soon be onshore, as depth decreased to under twelve fathoms. "Go ashore we must, and our only possible means of safety lay in driving her as hard and high on the beach as possible," according to Sears. At dawn, the *Orissa* found itself about three hundred yards off Nauset Beach. As Sears recalled:

> *Just then she struck with a shock, which threw everyone down on deck. A few heavy cold green seas passed over us. A few heavy seas on the quarter and broadside hove the ship onshore. The light spars were broken off by the shock. The life of the* Orissa *was ended.*

It wasn't long before a group of men, seeing the ship's situation, assembled on the beach, and soon a lifeboat was on the scene. Meanwhile, the *Orissa* crew assembled in the cabin and managed to consume a lunch of bread, sausage meat and brandy. Chief Officer Joseph Prentiss of Marblehead then led the effort to launch the ship's lifeboats. However, getting to shore was another matter—Prentiss and three other men never made it, but Sears and Captain William Lewis of Hyannis, the second mate, were among those who were hauled onto the beach by many willing hands.

The rescued were taken to the station for medical attention. Because of the snow, it was six days before they were taken to Yarmouth. Prentiss's body washed ashore in Chatham and was buried in Marblehead. Benjamin Best, a sailor, was found on shore in Chatham and buried there. The other bodies were never recovered. According to Edward Rowe Snow's *A Pilgrim Returns to Cape Cod*, Sears later said that Prentiss was a "gentleman and a good sailor" and that the storm in which the *Orissa* was lost was the greatest since Minot's Light in Scituate had crashed into the sea six years before.

The wreck of the *Orissa* continued to be a factor in people's lives for decades. The October 16, 1924 edition of the *Barnstable Patriot* referred to an 1894 report of "large quantities of copper and composition bolts" being retrieved from the ship's debris. As noted in the second volume of

The galley from the *Orissa* shipwreck is now part of the gift shop at the Church of the Holy Spirit in Orleans. *Church of the Holy Spirit.*

State Street Bank of Boston's *Town and City Seals of Massachusetts*, one of the quarter boards was salvaged and was in the collection at the State Street Bank main office. The lifesaving crew made a cane from the ship's teak wood decking and gave it to Sears, who was living in Baltimore. The deckhouse and galley were removed to form an ell to a house in South Orleans, now at the Church of the Holy Spirit. The cane's inscription read, "Ship *Orissa*, of Boston, wrecked January 18, 1857. Recovered from the wreck October, 1894, after having been buried thirty-seven years." Sears sent many gifts to Orissa Linnell for the rest of his life, including a set of dishes used in the *Orissa*'s passenger cabin.

In a 2016 interview, Orleans historian Bonnie Snow mentioned that "it took three weeks with thirty-two oxen for many men in town to unload the freight that was on the *Orissa*." Other cargo was also being collected and used many years later, according to State Street Bank:

> *For many years after the wreck of the* Orissa, *candied ginger and ginger tea from her cargo were common delicacies sparingly served in Orleans*

> *households. The phrase "full of ginger" was coined by envious out-of-towners in ribbing the energetic Orleans beachcombers.*

The *Orissa* continues to live on as part of the Church of the Holy Spirit in Orleans. Methodist priest Richard Kimball and his wife, Florence, lived in a house that was built from a section of the old Higgins Tavern, which dated back to the 1800s, as well as from the *Orissa*'s galley. The Kimballs referred to the house as "Galley West." The rest of the church's structure was gathered from the remains of the Chequesset Neck Inn in Wellfleet after it was destroyed in a storm.

CLARA BELLE

A SURVIVOR'S NIGHT OF DESPAIR

During the early morning hours of March 7, 1872, a North Truro farmer headed out to his stable to check on his animals, following a howling northeaster the night before. He then looked out at the road near the Highland House, where he spotted a half-dressed man, falling over from exhaustion and chilled to the bone.

The distressed man was John Silva, a sailor who, eight hours earlier, had been on board the coal-laden *Clara Belle* of Rockland, Maine, battling the gale-force winds on the open sea off Highland Light. The ship struck the sandbars off High Head, forcing the crew to abandon ship. "Believing she would break up at any minute, Captain Amesbury and six men dropped over their small boat, jumped in, and cast away," recalled historian Donald Trayser in the March 10, 1949 edition of the *Provincetown Advocate.* As Isaac M. Small recalled in his 1928 book, *Shipwrecks on Cape Cod*:

> *A great wave carried it high, and tumbled it over. Not two strokes of the oars had been taken when the cockleshell, borne like a chip on the top of an onrushing wave, was thrown bottom up and her crew was struggling in the icy waters. Captain Amesbury and one of his men were carried on a towering wave rapidly towards the shore, but before they could gain a foothold, the remorseless undertow had drawn them back into the swirling waters.*

Silva managed to grab a piece of wreckage and "by its aid managed to crawl away from the jaws of death," according to Small, but "in his struggles to reach the shore, one of his boots had been torn off and lost, he was coatless, without covering on his head, thoroughly drenched, his clothes freezing to his benumbed body and limbs." Silva was the only one to reach shore; his crew mates never had a chance. Once ashore, he was caught in the gale-force winds with temperatures below zero. He followed the direction of the wind and headed south, hoping to find shelter. As Small noted:

> *Over frozen fields, through brush and brambles that tore his bare foot at every step, over the ever increasing snow drifts, through bogs and meadows and hills and hollows, he struggled until the coming of daylight.*

Finally, Silva, whom Small described as being "so dazed by his terrible night of torture that he could not speak or move," was spotted by the farmer. Small, who was a marine reporting correspondent for the Boston Chamber of Commerce, was also on hand and assisted the farmer in reviving Silva, who had managed to wander three miles from the wreck. Silva would lose three toes and a finger to amputation, but he eventually recovered. While the women of the household cared for Silva, Small and the farmer headed for the wreck, which had been driven ashore by the waves. Small wrote:

> *We walked on board dry-footed and passed down the cabin stairs. There in the cabin stove burned a nice cheerful fire and all was dry and warm. The haste of Captain Amesbury and his crew to leave the strong vessel for a little frail skiff had cost them their lives.*

When the *Clara Belle* ran aground, the crew feared that the ship would break apart, so they opted to brave the high tide in the skiff. By morning, the boat was ashore. As Trayser noted, "Had all remained aboard the schooner, they could have stepped off four hours later without wetting their feet."

The Lifesavers of Cape Cod

Though starlight or buffeting storms, the yellow lantern will shine tonight along the beach. The man who carries it is well worthy of aid.
—Henry Beston, "The Wardens of Cape Cod," from World's Work Magazine, *1923*

Visiting the beach during a big storm and an Arctic blast is always an interesting experience on Cape Cod, but most have the option of ditching back into a warm car or house as soon as possible. The surfmen of the U.S. Life-Saving Service and the Coast Guard who patrolled the Outer Beach from 1872 until the 1940s didn't have a choice in the matter.

At one point, thirteen lifesaving (Coast Guard after 1915) stations lined the Cape's Outer Beach from Provincetown to Monomoy Island, the first being the Peaked Hill Station in Provincetown. Every night, except during the summer months, a surfman set out on a patrol, keeping an eye out for ships in distress and other activity on the Outer Beach—no matter what the weather conditions were. "Surfmen donned oils and, armed with a lantern, metal chits or a watchman's clock, and Coston signals, set out upon their rounds," wrote Dennis L. Noble in his book, *That Others Might Live*.

At any given station, beach patrols commenced at 4:30 p.m. The first patrol usually headed north, checked in at a halfway house that was located in between the stations, and then returned. Another patrol went out at 7:00 p.m., to the south, then continued every two and a half hours that way until sunrise. Imagine having to walk the beach, with the possibility of having to help execute an ice water–soaked rescue in the cards. Imagine driving sleet, wind, snow and sea spray. Then add in the uncertainty of having a constantly shifting surface under your feet, with the possibility of a rogue wave coming in at any minute. The worst natural opponent of all, according to many surfmen, was "the sand," as Henry Beston wrote in his book, *The Outermost House*:

> *My head turtled down into the very shoulders of my canvas coat, my eyes blinking and painful from the stabs of sand, my nostrils hot and dry with the breathing of it, my mouth much occupied in spitting out grits.*

Most of the shipwrecks occurred during the worst possible weather conditions—the tragedies of the *Montclair* (Orleans, 1927) and *Castagna* (Wellfleet, 1914) being classic examples of this. However, many other days and nights were very different. "Life at a station can be summed up very simply: hours and hours of boring routine, with always a chance for minutes of sheer terror," Noble wrote.

Many of these "Wardens of Cape Cod," in Beston's words, made the Life-Saving Service/Coast Guard their life's work. Some were forced into early retirement, often because of injuries and illnesses from the job, with no benefits. Others worked at it for a year or two and eventually opted for something else. Training for the job also wasn't an option, as longtime surfman Yngve Rongner, who started his extensive career in 1921, recalled for the Eastham Historical Society:

> *What I knew about the Coast Guard you could put into a twinkle! Didn't know the bow or stern of a boat or even how to row. I learned boat handling the hard way. No man that enlisted in those ever went to a boot camp for any training. Every day was a drill day, with instructions about boats, breeches buoys, resuscitation, saving a drowning person, International Code flags, semaphore, wigwag, flaming light* [Morse code], *storm signals, and also learning the book on Rules of the Road, some International laws, rules and regulations of the U.S. Coast Guard, and, oh yes, First Aid of all kinds.*

The surfmen patrolled the Outer Beach of Cape Cod beginning in 1872, as part of the U.S. Life-Saving Service and then as part of the Coast Guard after the Life-Saving Service and the Revenue Cutter Service were folded together in 1915. As Beston wrote in *World's Work Magazine*:

Above: Surfmen light a Coston flare on the beach, alerting both those aboard a stranded vessel and those on watch at the nearby lifesaving station. *Sturgis Library Archives.*

Right: From August until June, surfmen from the Cape Cod lifesaving stations patrolled the beaches from sunset to sunrise. *Sturgis Library Archives.*

It is the task of the surfmen to warn vessels standing into danger, to rescue them and their crews from positions of peril, to furnish fuel and food and water to ships in distress, and even, should occasion arise, to navigate a ship into the nearest port.

In a 2014 interview, novelist William Martin painted a picture of what a shipwreck rescue involved:

Somebody once said that if you could raise all the ships that have been sunk or run aground off the bars off of the Outer Beach, you could walk from Provincetown to Chatham without getting your feet wet, walking from ship to ship. When those ships would hit a bar, run aground, in the dark, in a storm, on a running tide, with a powerful northeast wind blowing in, they would suddenly become death traps for the men who were aboard them, and for the men who would have to go out and rescue them.

A surfman was typically a Cape Cod native and a skilled boatsman. While they often worked on drills and other necessary tasks during the daylight hours, it was during the night patrols where the job became more treacherous. From August to June, a lantern-laden surfman was sent out either to the north or south, where he would meet up with another station's surfman after walking for about four and a half miles. For instance, a Nauset Station surfman would meet up with the man from Cahoon Hollow to the north. Rongner described the nightly routine:

Night patrols and station watches were divided into five-hour shifts, with two men for each shift. One left to the north with his bag, holding a telephone, Costons and holder, and a time clock, over his shoulder.

High tides, particularly along the glacial cliffs, could leave a surfman with nowhere to run. The elements weren't the only hazard out there. During the 1920s, the Coast Guardsmen were often on the lookout for rumrunners, who were usually well armed. As J.W. Dalton wrote in his 1902 book, *The Life-Savers of Cape Cod*:

Death has often claimed the Life-Saver at his work. Or as a result of his gallant, unselfish toil for the safety of others in the rigors of winter, one Life-Saver after another is compelled to retire from the service on account of shattered health.

If wave conditions weren't too severe, surfmen would launch a surfboat from shore in an attempt to rescue those aboard a stranded vessel. *Cape Cod National Seashore.*

There were other perils the surfmen faced at night, although some of these tales were laughed about later. "One dark night returning to the station—what a surprise I got when two large paws landed on my shoulders!" Rongner recalled. It turned out to be a neighbor's Great Dane. Another time, he fell into a whale carcass that had washed ashore. "Boy, what an aroma!" he said. "You could smell me for miles!"

Rescue methods included rolling hand-rowed surfboats, which were dubbed "Race Point" and "Monomoy," out to vessels. These boats weighed between eight hundred and one thousand pounds. The other option was the breeches buoy, which involved firing a projectile to the boat, creating a sliding lifeline to shore. If the conditions weren't bad enough, the compensation could be somewhat meager. At the turn of the century, the pay was roughly $60 per month and went up to only $70 to $80 by the 1920s.

Dawn of the Life-Saving Service

Prior to 1872, the few inhabitants of this solitary stretch knew that the limited services of the Revenue Cutter Service were woefully inadequate to deal with the abundance of vessels running around on the outer bars. One of those residents, Sumner I. Kimball, was here for only a short time but would end up having a major influence on the establishment of the

USLSS. Kimball, a native of Maine, was a U.S. Treasury clerk and lawyer who was appointed as the chief of the Treasury Department's Revenue Marine Division in 1871. It was under his guidance that the USLSS was able to grow into the Coast Guard. According to the Orleans Historical Society, he worked briefly as a teacher in Orleans. As Edwin Emery wrote in *The History of Sanford, Maine*:

> *In his later youth* [Kimball] *was also witness to scenes around the ugly shores of Cape Cod, which were well calculated to intensify the earlier impressions; so that from this point of view alone there was much fitness that circumstances should afterwards so happen as to place him at the head of a great organization having for its splendid object the rescue of life from the perils of the sea.*

Kimball sent Captain John Faunce of the U.S. Revenue Marine on an inspection of the lifesaving network, which was particularly sparse on the Outer Cape. Faunce's report hardly painted a pretty picture, using the words *rusty* and *old* in describing both apparatus and personnel. Kimball turned out to be a bureaucratic genius, using Faunce's report and his own political savvy to get $200,000 from Congress to beef up the Life-Saving Service. "In what seems like lightning speed by today's standards, Kimball's efforts resulted in nine federally funded lifesaving stations on Cape Cod in 1872," wrote Ron Peterson in "The Lifesaving Legacy of Orleans" for the Orleans Historical Society. Those stations, part of District 2, were Chatham, Monomoy, Orleans, Nauset, Cahoon's Hollow, Pamet River, Highland, Peaked Hill Bars and Race Point and were manned by January 1873.

Kimball instituted six-man boat crews, drew up regulations with standards of performance for crew members, set station routines and set physical standards. By 1878, the formal establishment of the U.S. Life-Saving Service was signed into law by Congress, and Kimball would remain as its general superintendent until it was merged with the Coast Guard.

The USLSS was in dire need of improving its pay scales and working conditions, and Kimball, who could play the public relations game as well as anyone, succeeded in that quest. He hired William D. O'Connor, a professional author, to write the annual USLSS reports. In an October 2015 interview, Coast Guard historian Richard Boonisar said:

> *O'Connor would exaggerate the facts from the keepers' reports, but keep the facts the facts. Kimball would send these reports to Congress, and when he*

Left: Sumner I. Kimball, the first superintendent of the Life-Saving Service, worked briefly as a teacher in Orleans. *U.S. Coast Guard.*

Below: Surfmen were typically Cape Cod natives, such as most of the Nauset Station crew in 1901: George Snow, Charles Daniels, Orien Higgins, Whitman Howes, Warren Mayo, Allen Gill, Lewis Collins and Alonzo Bearse. *M.J. Stevenson.*

> *went for appropriations, Kimball was the ultimate federal bureaucrat in 1880s and '90s, and was the first to retire with a pension. These were written to be read. He got his money.*

O'Connor had little experience with maritime issues before joining the Treasury Department, which oversaw the Life-Saving Service. He first worked with the *Boston Commonwealth*, which Kimball described as "a prominent daily newspaper established for the advocacy of free-soil principles," in 1852 before moving on to Philadelphia. He worked in clerical jobs for the Lighthouse Board and the Treasury Department. Kimball wrote that O'Connor's descriptions were "couched in language at once so apt and graphic, with illustrations so vivid and fascinating as almost to make the stories real, present transactions taking place with all their heroism and horror within the reader's actual vision."

An example of O'Connor's "vivid and fascinating" details came in a description of a Provincetown wreck during January 1878: "The crew, in the water-soaked condition of their clothing, and exposed to the icy blast, they would have perished, the snowstorm completely preventing them from seeing what direction to take for refuge." He added that "in effecting the landing of these unfortunate men through such perils and difficulties, the fiery heroism of surfmen, so often seen upon our coast, was again manifest."

Paced by O'Connor's storytelling abilities, it was no wonder that Kimball was able to build the Life-Saving Service up, eventually leading to a pension for himself and, later, for members of the Coast Guard, which absorbed the Life-Saving Service in 1915.

O'Connor was also a painter and poet and was a friend of Walt Whitman, who said, "Other men are more famous...but no man is greater." O'Connor also wrote *The Good Gray Poet*, a defense of Whitman, which Kimball said exhibited "a complete mastery of every polemic weapon." O'Connor, however, would not live to see the Life-Saving Service become a part of the Coast Guard. He died in 1889 at the age of fifty-seven. As Kimball noted:

> *He brought...not only a mind richly stored with valuable attachments, but a heart full of the love of humanity, which through subsequent years he thoroughly dedicated to the great work entrusted to this department. How much the service owes to his untiring and loving fidelity none fully know save those most closely associated with him officially.*

Kimball died in Washington, D.C., in 1923, but his impact lived on, as USLSS historian Dennis Noble noted:

> *Kimball was unquestionably the driving force behind the United States' possessing a first-class lifesaving organization. Much of the present-day Coast Guard's highly regarded reputation as a humanitarian organization is the result of his organizational skills and management abilities.*

Long before the Cape Cod Canal made life so much easier for mariners, ships had to make their way around the outer bars of the peninsula. On many occasions, these ships ran aground, costing thousands of lives. That casualty total might have been even higher had it not been for the rescue efforts of the Life-Saving Service and the Coast Guard at the stations along the Outer Beach.

The tools of their trade were referred to as "beach apparatus." Among the items included were a breeches buoy, a Lyle gun (a small cannon), projectiles, a sand anchor and a faking box. These were all pulled down the beach in a cart by either the lifesaving crew, a horse or, in later years, a tractor. Surfmen patrolled the beach at night, one going north and another to the south. When a distressed ship was spotted, the surfman would light a Coston flare, which would summon those on watch at the nearby station and inform those on board the ship that help was on the way.

Oddly enough, surfmen faced another obstacle to their work when the "Great War" broke out in Europe during 1914. According to James Theriault's *Every First Monday*, Provincetown had its share of "super-patriots," who were indulging in what the author referred to as "witch hunts." The playwright Eugene O'Neill, who lived in the old Peaked Hill Bars Station after it was retired by the Coast Guard following World War I, was accused of signaling German vessels from a suitcase that turned out to be a typewriter. Theriault wrote that "members of the shore patrol routinely walking the beach at night with lanterns would be confronted with demands to know who they were signaling."

Rescues were made using either a surfboat or the breeches buoy if the surf were too high. The breeches buoy was a mortar with a projectile attached to a rope that got shot into the rigging of a sinking ship. The top was a lead-line that pulled a heavier rope, the pulley and the lifesaver ring all out to the ship. Once the lines were secured, the survivors could step into the legs of the breeches within the ring and be hauled ashore.

The crew from the Chatham Station run a breeches buoy drill. The breeches buoy was used when seas were too rough for a surfboat rescue. *Sturgis Library Archives.*

One of the earlier cannons used to fire projectiles from shore was the Hunt gun, but it was soon replaced by the Lyle gun (named for its inventor, Captain David Lyle). The Lyle gun fired a projectile out to five hundred yards, flying over the vessel, and dropped the line down to the crew, who pulled it aboard and attached it to a heavier whip line. In 1877, Lyle, a graduate of West Point and the Massachusetts Institute of Technology, was recruited by Life-Saving Service superintendent Sumner Kimball to develop a better line-throwing device. After two years, Lyle came up with a small 185-pound bronze cannon and carriage, capable of firing a seventeen-pound, fourteen-and-a-half-inch bullet-shaped projectile.

The line originated out of what was called a faking box. Attached to the line was a tally board, which provided instructions, in English and French, to the crew. The line would then be tied to the mast or other elevated spot on the vessel, creating a zip line between shore and ship, pulling in one sailor at a time. Proficiency was a must for surfmen when it came to setting up the breeches buoys. The best crews could fire the Lyle gun, rig a breeches buoy and haul a person down from the wreck pole in two minutes and thirty seconds. Crews had a five-minute limit to complete the drill. Failing to do so was cause for dismissal.

Nestled in between the stations were small huts known as "halfway houses." A Wellfleet-based halfway house, located between the Cahoon's Hollow and Pamet Stations, measured in at "eight feet by eight feet by twelve feet" and was likely built late in the nineteenth century, according

The Lyle gun, shown here with a surfboat at the Old Harbor Lifesaving Station Museum at Cape Cod National Seashore, was used to launch the breeches buoy. *Author's collection.*

to the October 17, 1968 edition of the *Cape Cod Standard-Times*. The paper described the structures, some of which may have served as refuge shacks for the Massachusetts Humane Society prior to the 1870s, as "the place where the patrolling surfmen from one station met to exchange brass checks with the patrols from the adjacent station, thus establishing that the patrol had been performed. Each man would then return to his own station with the check from the neighboring station some five miles away."

The surfmen were on patrol to keep watch for ships in distress out at sea or which had run aground on the sandbars a few hundred yards offshore. When a ship was spotted, surfmen would light a Coston flare to alert the ship's crew that help was coming and those on watch at the nearby stations. The halfway houses were tiny structures but were hooked up to a telephone system, which was often used to summon help. There would also be a coal stove for a quick warmup after the long walk through the severe winter conditions that often accompanied the ship disasters. During foul weather, the patrols were exhausting. Surfmen often had to hold a wooden shingle or a folded newspaper in front of their faces to keep the sand out of their eyes.

The fate of many of the huts is unknown, although the halfway house between Pamet and Cahoon's Hollow was salvaged in October 1968. Thanks to a deal brokered by curator Edmund Lynch of the Marine Historical Association, former Cape Cod National Seashore superintendent Stanley Joseph and Major Frederick Cameron, USMC, of the South Weymouth Naval Air Station, the hut, isolated and half buried in the sand, was lifted off the eroding dune by a naval helicopter. "Its

Surfmen patrolling the outer beach often met up at "halfway houses," which offered shelter and were equipped with telephones. *Cape Cod National Seashore.*

method of removal required months of study before the final decision was made to lift it out by helicopter," the *Standard-Times* reported.

It took three days to prepare the hut for airlift. It was removed from its base and wood footings and then, using cables, blocks and tackle, careened on its side. "A cable surrounding the halfway house was secured to a hook on the plane's underside, and the building was then picked up and carried approximately a mile to a parking lot and deposited on the flat trailer which was waiting there to bring it to Mystic Seaport."

Today, few reminders of those lifesaving outposts remain on the Outer Beach. Most of them have been claimed by the sand and sea, much like the surfmen who utilized them. The Cahoon's Hollow Station in Wellfleet is now the Beachcomber, a popular nightclub and restaurant. The second Nauset Station is now a Cape Cod National Seashore educational facility. Chatham's Old Harbor Station now sits on the high dunes of Race Point in Provincetown and serves as a Cape Cod National Seashore museum. The poison ivy–covered ruins of the second Peaked Hill Bars Station and the High Head Station remain in the dunes of North Truro and Provincetown.

Thanks to the surfmen and their expertise with the rescue apparatus, many of those who would have been lost at sea survived to see another day. Earle Rich offered this take in his book, *Cape Cod Echoes*:

> *They were, in my opinion, the last of a breed. Come hell or high water and with utter disregard for their own safety, the safety of a shipwrecked sailor clinging to the rigging of some stranded vessel came above all else to them.*

FRANCES

A VOLUNTEER RESCUE

Following the establishment of the U.S. Life-Saving Service in 1872, government officials began the mad rush of building rescue stations along Cape Cod's east-facing shoreline. As the year ended, appointments had been made, but outside of a few Humane Society structures and equipment, not much else was in place.

In Truro, Edwin Worthen, thirty-six, was appointed as the first keeper at the Highland Station on December 12, 1872, but when the *Frances*, a German bark carrying a load of sugar from India, ran aground along what is now known as Head of the Meadow Beach on December 26, there was no one to turn to immediately. Upon arrival at the beach, several crew sailors were clinging to the rigging, nearly frozen. Worthen's obituary in the June 26, 1909 edition of the *Yarmouth Register* detailed his rescue mission:

> *Keeper Worthen raised a volunteer crew, requisitioned an old whaleboat, which the men hauled through the deep snow drifts in the teeth of one of the fiercest gales of winter to a point abreast the wreck, two miles from the starting point. Four separate times that forenoon, with four fresh men each time at the oars, Captain Worthen made trips to the vessel and the men of the* Frances *were saved by the courage and skill of the newly-appointed keeper and his followers.*

Fortunately for the crew, everyone survived the ordeal, but the ship's master, Captain Wilhelm Kortling, had been ill and died shortly after the

Edwin Worthen, *left*, was the newly appointed keeper of the Highland Station in Truro in 1872, when the *Frances* ran aground. He retired in 1907. *Cape Cod National Seashore.*

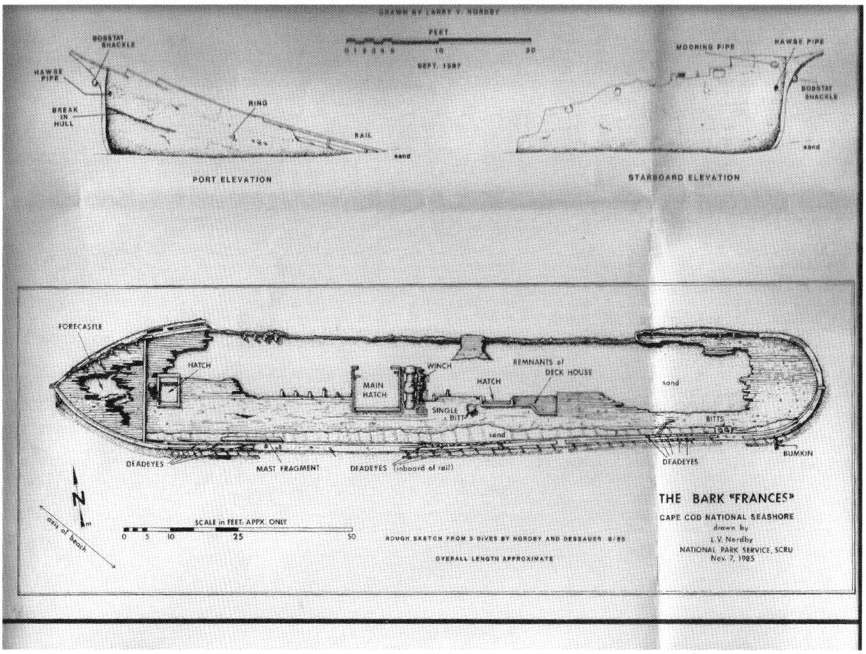

An illustration of the interior of the German bark *Frances*, which stranded on Head of the Meadow Beach in North Truro in December 1872. *Cape Cod National Seashore.*

The remains of the bark *Frances* can often be seen at low tide along Head of the Meadow Beach in North Truro. *Cape Cod National Seashore.*

rescue at the Highland House. He was buried nearby. Worthen was still tending to the captain's grave when he retired due to ill health in 1907. The veteran keeper died two years later.

The *Frances* was carrying loads of sugar in straw mats. Many of locals who were salvaging the wreck were able to "secure a year's supply of sugar for their families," according to Isaac M. Small.

The crew of the *Frances* was spared the full wrath of the sea. The *Peruvian*, which was within sight of the *Frances* for most of the journey from India, would not be so fortunate.

PERUVIAN

A DREAM DESTROYED

Only those who have been suddenly overwhelmed with a paralyzing blow can appreciate what, with ruined hopes, this young girl felt, when she opened the daily paper only to read in great black, cruel headline these words, "Ship Peruvian *goes down off Cape Cod, and all hands are lost."*
—Isaac M. Small, Shipwrecks of Cape Cod, *1928*

During the final weeks of 1872, a young woman in the mountains of New Hampshire was anxiously awaiting the return of her fiancé, Captain Zina Vannah, who was on his final voyage at sea. The couple was to be married shortly after. Vannah, twenty-eight, was the captain of the bark *Peruvian*, which was heading back to Boston from India. Before departing, Vannah sent a letter, advising her as to when he would arrive in Boston. She was headed to the city to greet him.

Alas, the *Peruvian* never made it. Trying to maneuver its way through a vicious northeaster, the *Peruvian* was no match for the driving snow, high winds and towering waves and ran aground on the Peaked Hill Bars, about one mile off the shore of Provincetown. Small's description read as follows:

> *The men climbed into the masts, but it was soon overcome by a massive wave. The entire crew was hurled into this mass of thrashing wreckage and churning sea, and their last sad cries were hushed in the mad seas that covered them.*

Captain Zina Vannah and his crew all perished aboard the *Peruvian* in December 1872. Vannah had promised his fiancée that this would be his final voyage. *Jim Bickford.*

The *Peruvian* was one of two vessels to run aground that night. Three miles away, the German bark *Frances* was stranded near what is now Head of the Meadow Beach in Truro. The *Peruvian* lost all twenty-two members of its crew, while a rescue mission managed to save all of the men aboard the *Frances*. According to the December 25, 1930 edition of the *Hyannis Patriot*:

> *The* Frances *and* Peruvian *sailed from Calcutta and were in sight of each other every day until that night. The* Peruvian *load consisted of raw sugar, crude rubber, rattans, and block tin. Some time later a diver recovered $20,000 worth of tin. The tin was from the mines in India, moulded into blocks of one hundred pounds each.*

The rubber and rattans began washing ashore shortly thereafter. The January 1, 1873 edition of the *Provincetown Advocate* reported:

> *The* Peruvian *lies in fragments for five miles along the shore. Her clock, which was picked up, had stopped at 10 minutes past four. The wreckers say that pieces of the wreck began to come ashore at midnight Thursday*

> *night. Up to Tuesday morning four bodies had been found, one being the mate's, Mr. Baine, and one a child's, about nine years old. Children's clothes were also found.*

As Small noted, Vannah, "a seafaring man all his life," and his bride-to-be "had planned when his sea voyages were ended he would come to claim his bride and would sail the sea no more. He had secured a fair competency and had promised her that this would be his last voyage."

GIOVANNI

"A MELANCHOLY DISASTER"

It was one of those terrible marine disasters, of which there are many, where man is a plaything in the grip of the sea where the storm king is abroad in his might.
—Isaac M. Small, Shipwrecks on Cape Cod, *1928*

During the late afternoon and evening hours of March 4, 1875, the Italian bark *Giovanni* ran aground during a storm on the outer bar of Cape Cod, three miles west of the Highland Life-Saving Station in Truro. Thirteen men perished in the tragedy.

Yet what was on board the wrecked vessel, bound for Boston from Palermo, Italy, may have led to even more deaths across the Cape tip area, according to a report/editorial in the *Provincetown Advocate* the following week. The ship carried a large haul of cargo that happened to include "a number of casks of claret and other wines." According to the *Advocate*:

> *Many of these casks were cut into and the heads knocked out and men in a disgustingly gluttonous manner gorged themselves with the contents till they became intoxicated, several cases resulting fatally it is reported, while others appeared in town so drunk that they needed the walk widened in order to save their jugs and demijohns from being smashed against the iron fences.*

The fact that word of this alcoholic binge reached beyond the borders of the Outer Cape seemed to annoy the *Advocate*'s editor even further:

> *If these stories were confined here and affected the reputation of only those who deserved censure the case would present a pleasanter aspect, but last week the city dailies gave an account of the disgraceful affair. We believe there is no place or time at which human weaknesses become so conspicuous as at a shipwreck.*

The *Giovanni* found itself caught up in an unmanageable maelstrom before stranding "upon the outer edge of the inner bar," according to the *Advocate*. Crews from both the High Head and Highland Stations, under the leadership of Keepers David Atkins and Edwin Worthen, respectively, made attempts at a rescue. However, sending out a surfboat wasn't possible due to the rough seas, and the force of the wind shut down the possibility of using the breeches buoy.

By evening, three men on board the ship tried to float ashore on planks. Two of them perished in the attempt, but one was saved by Bernard Jason, who was on the beach. Jason had a line, waded into the surf and managed to pull the man ashore. "That a human being could live through such a night as that, in that icy water and retain his hold upon any part of those ice covered timbers and sea-swept wreck seemed incredible," wrote Isaac M. Small in *Shipwrecks on Cape Cod*.

The *Giovanni* was one of the more than three thousand shipwrecks on Cape Cod's Outer Bar, but the loss of life on the beach—and the bizarre aftermath—left many on the Cape Tip scarred. The wreck "has proved one of the most melancholy disasters that have ever occurred upon our coast," the *Advocate* wrote. "Those upon the beach describe the scene before the vessel broke entirely up, with the men clinging to the rigging, as truly heart rending."

As far as the wreckers were concerned, the *Advocate* didn't feel that history would look favorably on their behavior:

> *To witness the greedy and rapacious manner with which some of the habitués of the terrible scenes pounce upon and seize everything of value that appears in the surf even before the waves have given up the rightful custodians and owners, tends to convince the spectator that all traces of barbarousness are not yet obliterated.*

The ship also contained 200 tons of brimstone, 300 bales of rags, 200 bags of filberts and 4,925 bags of Pojero sumac. There was also $70,000 in gold. Several bodies, including the captain's, eventually washed ashore.

Truro's Triple Wreck of 1878

The loss of life awakens one to a peculiar sense of what he is and how frail and weak is his earthly bark.
—Provincetown Advocate, *January 10, 1878*

When the call of "vessel ashore!" rang out at one of the thirteen lifesaving stations along Cape Cod's Outer Beach during the late nineteenth century, it often took every resource that the surfmen could tap into for the rescue efforts. So one can just imagine how taxing it was on the men from the Pamet River Station during the early morning hours of January 3, 1878, when not one, not two, but *three* vessels struck the outer bar, all within minutes and under a mile from one another.

Out of the three vessels, twenty-one men were saved, while twelve perished in the raging surf, stirred up by a storm that came on "very sudden and unexpected," according to the January 10, 1878 edition of the *Provincetown Advocate*. Keeper Nelson Weston of the Pamet Station found himself having to prioritize rescue efforts in a hurry. One half mile to the south, the *Pow-Wow*, captained by Matthew Eaton of Provincetown, and later the *Miles Standish*, another Cape tip vessel, both struck the bar, while to the north, the *Addie M. Avery* was in a similar situation. "Weston, was for a moment, greatly embarrassed in regard to the course to be pursued, two vessels, with crews in peril, being simultaneously on shore in opposite directions, help being possible to only one of them at a time," wrote the Life-Saving Service's William D. O'Connor in his 1904 collection, *Heroes of the Storm*.

With the crew of the *Pow-Wow* having fifteen men in distress, the rescue effort began there. A line was shot in an attempt to utilize a breeches buoy rescue, but the crew was unable to fasten the line to the boat. In an effort to make the best of a bad situation, the line was tied around the waists of crew members, and one at a time, men were dragged through the raging surf to shore. As O'Connor noted:

> *This desperate measure, which necessity compelled, was rendered even more dangerous by the terrible character of the surf and by the presence in the tumultuous water of fragments of timbers, spars, and planking from the vessel, capable of inflicting the worst bruises and fatal wounds, and, worse still, of masses of tangled and writhing cordage, forming the most perilous of snares for one struggling through the breakers.*

The surfmen, with cords tied around their waists, "would go deep into the fearful undertow to aid them." Ten of the fifteen crew members were hauled in this way, but the last sailor was caught "in the wreckage of the jib," and two surfmen attempted to free him. One of those men was Ephraim Dyer, a veteran surfman from Truro. Dyer "became entangled in the wreckage of one of the vessels, and a big rope, becoming twisted around his legs, dragged him to the bottom, nearly drowning him," wrote J.W. Dalton in his 1902 book, *The Lifesavers of Cape Cod*. At this point, another surfman, "with incredible hardihood, rushed into the boiling surf with his knife and cut them free by severing the line beyond them," O'Connor wrote. "This daring feat, necessary for the safety of the three men, involved the sacrifice of the connection thus far maintained with the vessel."

One more man onboard had a line thrown to him, but his lifeless body dropped into the sea. Prior to this, one man had fallen from the bowsprit exhausted, and a boy froze to death. Before the lifesavers arrived, when the vessel first struck, the captain and another man fell overboard and drowned.

Six men aboard the *Avery* would not be as fortunate. Indications were that the *Avery* had broken up when it struck. The crew of the *Miles Standish* was close enough to shore that the men were able to get to land without assistance. They were taken to the station and provided with dry clothing, and several of them assisted in the *Pow-Wow* rescue effort.

Crowds gathered along the beach after the storm. As the *Advocate* opined, "The beach is constantly patrolled by the station men, expecting every hour a corpse to be washed ashore."

SARAH J. FORT

RETURN OF A RESCUER WHALEBOAT

[The wreck of the *Sarah J. Fort*] *has brought before the public the pressing need of light, handy surf boats.*
—Yarmouth Register, *April 19, 1879*

In 1856, Isaac F. Mayo of Provincetown was involved in the rescue of men from the stranded schooner *Clarendon*. It was a whaleboat that he and several other Massachusetts Humane Society volunteers utilized in their heroic deed. Twenty-three years later, Captain Mayo returned to lifesaving work when the three-master schooner *Sarah J. Fort* of Tuckerton, New Jersey, struck the Peaked Hill Bars off Provincetown. As it was reported in the April 15, 1912 edition of the *Barnstable Patriot*, "in the same boat with which he and his followers saved the men of the *Clarendon*, he performed the crowning feat of a series of brave deeds, by steering his volunteer crew safely through the Peaked Hill breakers and effecting the rescue of men of the three-master *Sarah J. Fort*."

Mayo and several other volunteers took to Provincetown's back shore on April 4, 1879, to relieve the exhausted surfmen from the Peaked Hill, Race Point and Highland Stations. According to the *Patriot*, the crews from the lifesaving stations "had unavailingly labored for a period of nine hours, during which period of time their own boat was twice filled with water and cast back upon the beach, suffering serious injury." Two men perished before the surfmen were able to reach the *Sarah J. Fort*.

The coal-laden *Sarah J. Fort* was heading to Boston from Hoboken, New Jersey, before it ran into trouble during a storm off the Cape and struck the bar around 1:00 a.m., due to what the U.S. Life-Saving Service concluded what was "an error in navigation." Two patrolmen from the Peaked Hill Station were out on patrol and came across wreckage washing ashore, but they assumed it was from a wreck off Scituate a few days earlier. They returned to the station to report their findings and resumed their patrols.

Two hours later, pieces of a boat and deck-plank were spotted. Shrouded in darkness, the surfmen were able to spot the distressed vessel in the water and returned to the station to alert Keeper David Atkins.

The rescue mission was hampered from the start. As the Life-Saving Service noted, "The sand, converted by the snow and surf into a species of slush, was in terrible condition for hauling." At this point, stations didn't have horses to help haul their apparatus to wreckage sites. This one was more than a mile from the station.

The Peaked Hill Station had a brand-new tool in its apparatus cart: the Lyle gun, a small cannon used for firing lines via projectiles to stranded vessels offshore. Atkins determined that the vessel was too far offshore to use the new cannon, so they retrieved the Parrott gun, a heavier device with a broader range. As the Life-Saving Service later noted, "This was a grievous error, only extenuated by the circumstance that the Lyle gun had been recently supplied to the station, and its powers had not become apprehended."

On his way back to the station, Atkins came across a man with a horse and cart, and they were engaged to pull the station's surfboat and equipment to the site. Between 4:30 a.m. and 5:30 a.m., Atkins, along with crews from Keeper Edwin Worthen's Highland Station and the Race Point Station (Keeper Young), were there to offer assistance. However, the tide and surf were way too high for a boat rescue at this point. The Life-Saving Service noted that "the schooner's hull was almost buried in the water, which perpetually rushed over her, and her crew of six men, including the captain, were up in the fore-rigging, clinging for life."

By 7:00 a.m., the mizzenmasts of the *Sarah J. Fort* had collapsed. Nine shots were fired from the Parrott gun, none of which was successful. The Life-Saving Service noted:

> *The firing was directly in the wind's eye, and the lines either fell short or were snapped by heavy charges of powder employed to strain the gun's carrying power to the utmost.*

As the morning wore on, the foremast of the *Fort* fell, but the tide had also ebbed, giving the surfmen an opportunity to launch the surfboat. The men of the *Fort*, who were clinging to life in the masts, were able to "leave the rigging of the fallen spar, and huddle together in the port bow," according to the Life-Saving Service. This part of the wreck was partially submerged, while parts of the ship continued to break up. The agency noted that at about 10:00 a.m., "while all hands were yet in the rigging, the cook fell into the sea from exhaustion, and perished, and shortly after the mate also. The survivors in the port bow were four." For the surfboat launch, four men were recruited from Peaked Hill Station, with three more from Highland. As the Life-Saving Service reported:

> *To these were added Captain Isaac F. Mayo of Provincetown, a surfman of great experience and bravery, who had come upon the beach with a number of citizens from Provincetown, drawn by the news of a wreck, and now begged permission to be taken in with the crew as a volunteer.*

The first two attempts resulted in the boat filling up with water, and on the second return trip, a large wave pushed the boat on to the shore, "springing five of her timbers and splitting her garboard." Fortunately for the men, they were able to make it to shore, but the boat was damaged on impact. As time was already limited, repairing the boat was out of the question.

Fortunately for the rescue party, another boat was at their disposal. Captain Harvey Cook had just driven a buggy onto the beach and took Keeper Atkins back into town to secure an old whaleboat, used by Mayo two decades earlier. It was a different and smaller model, which turned out to be favorable for the rescue. It was at this point that the veteran Mayo took over, according to the Life-Saving Service:

> *Captain Mayo, to whose charge she appears to have been consigned, assumed command and chose a crew of fresh men for her, declining to receive on board Keeper Atkins and several members of his crew who pleaded to be allowed to go. In taking this course, Captain Mayo was undoubtedly justified. The keeper and his men having eaten nothing since the evening before, and being much spent by their exertions since about 3 a.m., and their long exposure upon the wintry beach, could not reasonably be preferred by the leader of a volunteer effort, to an unworn crew.*

Two more attempts were made with the whaleboat, but this time they were able to get past the first bar. Here they were met with "masses of wreck debris, snarls of cordage, wefts of canvas, broken planks and timbers convulsively diving and tumbling on every side." Somehow, Mayo and his charges managed to navigate their way to the vessel. One by one, the four men, whose lives were close to slipping away, were removed and rowed to shore, but as the Life-Saving Service noted, there was still one more hurdle to overcome, as a heavy wave overtook the boat and spilled its occupants into the incoming surf and undertow:

> *An instantaneous rush was made by all on shore, and the people were seized by scores of hands and dragged from the water. Some were under the boat, and all were in imminent danger of being swept away and drowned. It is fortunate that the great crowd of spectators present made abundant assistance available, as otherwise loss of life would probably have ensued.*

The rescued men—cold, frostbitten and exhausted—were taken to the Peaked Hill Station. The wives of Atkins and Mayo had food prepared for them and dressed the shipwreck victims' frostbitten hands. Two of the rescued men remained at the station for four days.

Mayo was honored with a gold medal from the Life-Saving Service, while he and the rescue boat crew were all awarded silver medals from the Massachusetts Humane Society. Mayo received one more honor later that year. According to the September 9, 1879 edition of the *Barnstable Patriot*, "memorial of the gallantry of Capt. Isaac F. Mayo and his crew, has been hung in the public library at Provincetown. In the centre is a view of the scene, painted by John L. Ryder."

Mayo, along with his wife and grandson, didn't remain in Provincetown long. They moved to North Dakota later that year and took up farming, never to return to the Cape. He died thirty-three years later on April 5, 1912. The efforts of Atkins, however, were not looked on as favorably by the Life-Saving Service:

> *He has always been regarded as an efficient keeper, and his record for fidelity, courage, and energy at scenes of shipwreck, is known to the officers of the service. The Lyle gun would probably have established the desired line communication with the wreck, and his failure to employ it, through a strange in apprehension of its merits, must be deplored.*

The nightmares, however, for Atkins were just beginning.

C.E. Trumbull

Rescuers Lost

Sam Fisher and Charles Kelley were the only ones to reach the shore, following an heroic struggle, encouraged by the beams of a lantern in the hands of surfman John Cole.
—Admiral Donald McMillan

Unfortunately, many surfmen from the U.S. Life-Saving Service didn't come back between 1872 and the years leading up to World War II, especially when there were instances where an attempt wasn't completely necessary. This was the case in the wreck of the *C.E. Trumbull* on November 30, 1880, when the Maine sloop, carrying a load of granite, ran aground a mile south of the Peaked Hill Bars Life-Saving Station in Provincetown.

Three surfmen, including Keeper David Atkins from the Peaked Hills Station, perished trying to save the lives of the Trumbull crew. According to Donald Trayser's historical account in the December 2, 1948 edition of the *Provincetown Advocate*:

> *Captain Atkins and his men got safely alongside the sloop through angry seas and called on the crew to jump. One by one, four jumped into the surfboat; two, Captain Elwell and Pilot Pool, didn't. There were two versions why they didn't—one that the captain wanted to save his clothes and valuables, the other that he and the pilot refused to take a chance jumping.*

A Life-Saving Service surfboat made it to the distressed sloop *C.E. Trumbull*, but three surfmen perished in the rescue attempt. *Cape Cod National Seashore.*

Years later, surfman Isaiah Young recalled for the September 4, 1904 edition of the *Boston Globe*: "We went off and took [the men ashore]—the others refusing to leave without their personal effects."

"The captain and the mate refused to take the chance, thus making it necessary for Captain Atkins and his men to return to the shore," wrote Isaac M. Small in his 1928 book, *Shipwrecks on Cape Cod.*

The surfboat, making a second attempt to rescue the other two men, had six men aboard—Atkins, Elisha Taylor, Stephen Mayo, Charles P. Kelley, Samuel O. Fisher and Young. According to Trayser, as the lifeboat neared the sloop, the boom caught the bow of the lifeboat and capsized it. "Atkins, Surfmen Taylor and Mayo hung on until icy waters loosened their grips and they disappeared in the deep," Trayser wrote. As the men clung to the toppled boat, Young asked Mayo for a chew of tobacco. As Young recalled for the *Boston Globe*:

> *He passed me a piece without speaking. I bit off a chew and then put the remainder in my pocket. I have that bit of tobacco yet—a memento, 'tis of the most trying hour of my life.*

The men knew that they had few options, so they made an effort to get to the beach. As Small wrote:

> *Young, Kelley, and Fisher, who were good swimmers, seeing that if they clung much longer to the boat must soon go as had their mates before them, so kicking off rubber boots and as much clothing as they could, struck out boldly for shore, which they reached exhausted and chilled, and were pulled from the surf.*

The bodies of Atkins, Taylor and Mayo were recovered later that day. Atkins's body was recovered by men from the nearby Highland Station in Truro, one of them being the Peaked Hill keeper's son. The *Trumbull* "sailed away with captain and pilot on board," as Trayser noted, and "drifted down and anchored near Chatham Bars," according to the December 7, 1880 edition of the *Chatham Monitor*. "She was supplied with a jib and three men—Josiah Hardy, Charles Hammond, and Samuel Dill—who went with her to Boston."

A few years later, Kelley was appointed as the keeper at the new High Head Station in North Truro, a position he held for twenty years. According to James Theriault's book *Every First Monday*, Kelley was later involved with rescues of the schooners *Laura Brown*, *Oliver Ames*, *Plymouth Rock*, *Red Rover*, *Lucia Porter*, *Abbie H. Hodgman*, *Job H. Jackson* and *Carrie Richardson*, all of which were total wrecks.

As for Young, the ordeal "unfitted me for further lifesaving work," he told the *Globe*. "One of my legs was practically useless for nearly two years, and it has been a source of trouble to me ever since."

However, the fact that the two men on the *Trumbull* refused to jump will forever hang over this deadly affair. As Trayser put it, if Atkins "hadn't been compelled by a sense of duty to make a second trip to the stranded sloop, the tragedy would not have happened."

J.H. Eells

An Unexpected Rescue

The circumstances of the failure of the Lifesaving crew to render any important service at this wreck were very thoroughly inquired into. The weight of the testimony taken points very clearly to the fact that the conditions of the wind, the sea, and the current, as well as the great distance of the wreck from the shore, were entirely against the chances for successful operations.
—U.S. Life-Saving Service Annual Report, *1888*

Every so often, the elements would get in the way of a rescue attempt by the U.S. Life-Saving Service. This was the case during the wreck of the schooner *J.H. Eells* near the Nauset Station on March 15, 1887. Fortunately for the survivors, a Boston tugboat came to the rescue in just the nick of time.

Two men perished during the wreck of the *J.H. Eells*, which inspired Joseph Lincoln's book *Rugged Water*. The *Rockport*, a Maine-based schooner under the command of Captain Frederick Wallace, was heading from Perth Amboy, New Jersey, to Boston carrying a load of railroad and pig iron when a snowstorm, with northwesterly gales, kicked in as the vessel was passing Cape Cod. The weather conditions, according to the Life-Saving Service annual report, "compelled her to turn about and run for the nearest shelter down the coast. Skirting the shore too closely and steering wildly, for she had already sprung a leak."

At about 9:00 a.m. on March 15, Keeper Walter Knowles of the Nauset Station briefly spotted the vessel at sea. "I could just see the vessel through the thick snow running south close to the outer bar under a reefed foresail," Knowles wrote in his report. "About this time the vessel jibed inshore." Knowles and a surfman ran out to the beach, and "she jibed again with the apparent intention of keeping offshore." Knowles tried to follow the vessel through the poor visibility but lost it.

After Knowles's return to the station, surfmen Alonzo Bearse, who was on the north patrol, and O.C. Smith, out to the south, soon returned as well. Smith reported the vessel ashore about a mile and a half to the south. Knowles and the crew, with a surfboat in tow, arrived at the scene around 10:00 a.m. The Life-Saving Service report detailed what they found:

> *There was a very rough sea tumbling in about the vessel, notwithstanding the lowness of the tide, and at times the waves would break over the stern and sweep the deck from one end to the other. This could plainly be seen from shore.*

Preparations were made quickly. At 10:30 a.m., the first launch got off, but within thirty or forty yards of the schooner's bow, the full force of the powerful current alongshore was encountered and the boat was swept southward. Several more attempts were made but failed, hampered by the rising tide. At this point, Knowles opted for a breeches buoy, and four men were sent back to the station. They returned with the Lyle gun around 11:30 a.m., and eleven shots were attempted. Not one of them was successful, as the Life-Saving Service annual report noted:

> *Seven* [attempts] *failed to reach the mark, and the remaining four broke the lines in twain. Strange to say, in none of these shots did the keeper employ the lighter, or No. 4 line, which would certainly have reached the vessel, as it did when subsequently used with the Hunt gun at an even greater distance.*

More assistance began to arrive at the scene, including Life-Saving Service district superintendent Benjamin Sparrow of Orleans, who had been ill and bedridden. Also on hand was Captain Jabez Snow of the Massachusetts Humane Society, who was equipped with a Hunt gun. The deck of the schooner was now submerged, and the beach was also covered to the foot of the bluff, forcing the rescuers and their gun to higher ground. This put the crew at four hundred yards from the wreck. Two shot attempts failed, and as the Life-Saving Service noted:

> *Captain Snow then proposed that Keeper Knowles should fire it in his own way. The latter therefore increased the charge from three to six ounces of Service powder, and with that shot laid the line, a No. 4, between the schooner's masts and just above the three men in the starboard fore rigging.*

Even though this was the most success that the rescuers had up to this point, it was short-lived. The current proved to be too much for the line, "and communication was severed with the wreck," the agency report said. "The day was now far spent and darkness was coming on." Further rescue attempts had to wait until morning.

All four men were in the rigging at this point, and the exposure and adverse conditions were beginning to take their toll. By morning, two of the three men in the crosstrees were alive, the other having died from exposure. Captain Wallace, who had gone out on the bowsprit for a while before retreating back to the masts, was washed overboard shortly after midnight. Rescuing the remaining two men looked hopeless, but just then, the Boston tug *Underwriter* came into sight, according to the Life-Saving Service report:

> *She quickly ran in as close as possible in answer to a signal from the bluff and lowered a boat, which, watching its chances, was skillfully headed in for the wreck. The movements of the boat were watched with breathless interest from the shore, and when it gallantly reached the bow of the vessel and was seen to take off the two survivors, who managed to slide down the jib-stay to the bowsprit and thence dropped into the boat, a glad shout of approval went up from the assembled multitude.*

The two men were Swedes, one being the mate, John Olsen. They were exhausted from exposure and hunger and badly frostbitten. They couldn't be landed anywhere locally due to the rough surf, so they were taken to Boston. "The lifeless body in the rigging was left on the wreck, as the sea continued heavy through the day, the body could not be reached," Knowles wrote. It wasn't until the next day that the rescuers were able to get a boat out to the wreck and retrieve the body. "The limbs were badly frozen and the body thinly clad," the Nauset keeper added.

The arrival of the *Underwriter* proved to be the difference in saving the two men, even though the Life-Saving Service concluded that the surfmen, and the many others who assisted them, did everything in their power to rescue the crew of the *J.H. Eells*:

The current was in fact so strong, according to the statement of one eye witness, that when the whip line bowed out to its full scope in the water to the leeward, fifty stout men pulling with all their might were at times unable to gain a step to the windward in their efforts to lighten the task of the two men in the schooner's cross trees. The people being thus practically cut off for the time being from any prospect of rescue shoreward, it was indeed providential and a matter for profound congratulation that the Underwriter *arrived so opportunely and released the survivors, who otherwise in a few hours must have perished.*

Catboat Rescue at Crab Ledge

Even though it happened long ago, Captain Doane's rescue of his comrades of the sea is a highlight of a hardy and courageous era that the Chatham folk—the younger ones as well as the adults—want to remember and respect.
—Cape Codder, *November 18, 1948*

During the late nineteenth and early twentieth centuries, Captain Alonzo I. Doane of Chatham spent a good deal of his time on the water, whether it was pleasure boating or towboating or with the U.S. Life-Saving Service. So when he and Fred Nickerson were caught up in rough seas on March 19, 1891, near Crab Ledge, about ten miles off Chatham Bars, they still managed to rescue two other fishermen whose catboat had capsized. Because of his bravery, Doane was awarded a medal by the Massachusetts Humane Society.

Fishing boats were out in abundance that day, but as wind speeds increased, many opted to return to port. Doane and Nickerson, along with another catboat manned by George Nickerson and Rufus Nickerson, stayed at sea, hoping for "a better catch," but worsening conditions sent them back toward shore as well. After a while, Doane lost sight of the other boat and back out they went, sensing trouble. He told his story to the *Cape Codder* for the newspaper's November 18, 1948 edition:

We got there and found the sea had took him and capsized him. She sank pretty quick. We were away 15 minutes, that's all. We had to make another

> *tack to get them. Lucky we had a fair wind. Couldn't see the boat. Made another tack to stand to the north where she should be. Those seas were bad. Then I saw the two buckets. Turned out to be the heads of the two men.*

Fortunately, the cabin retained enough air to keep the boat afloat, according to Doane:

> *When we got up to where those two heads were, then we had to make another tack to get alongside those stays and take them off. Bowsprit was dipping down. That first tack meant everything. If we hadn't got up on that first tack we'd lost them. For she sank five minutes after we go them aboard our boat.*

Doane then said that their troubles didn't end there. When they got the men aboard, all were in danger. Capsizing was a big concern until they all made it over the Chatham bar:

> *When we hauled them aboard they had plenty of water in 'em. Rufus had more water in him. He had a grip on that stay that was like a death grip. He was pretty far gone. I had to wrench his hand off as we came up quickly and took them off. Pretty close call for Rufus. While we were working on 'em, George kept saying, "Never mind about us, you two watch your boat."*

Fifty-seven years after the incident, Doane still couldn't believe his good luck in moving alongside the distressed vessel without finding themselves in a similar situation. "If it wasn't for the experience we had and knowing what to do in a few quick moments we'd all been lost."

Jason

A Hopeless Disaster

None of the men…even so much as entertained the thought of attempting to launch the boat. It was out of question, absolutely and beyond all possibility of cavil.
—U.S. Life-Saving Service Annual Report, *1894*

Over the long history of shipwrecks on the Outer Beach of Cape Cod, there have been occasions where the term "sole survivor" can be applied to members of a lost vessel. This situation certainly applied on December 5, 1893, when the British ship *Jason* ran aground on the sandbars near the Pamet River Station in Truro.

Samuel J. Evans of Raglan, England, was the only member of the twenty-six-man crew who lived through the ordeal. Evans, an apprentice clad in a life preserver, tossed about in the waves after the ship struck the bars, clung to a bale of jute and managed to get to the beach, where he struggled ashore toward the lantern of a Pamet Station surfman. The *Jason* had been at sea for ten months, setting sail for Boston from Calcutta, India, on February 15. The 1,512-ton ship, loaded with ten thousand bales of jute, barely survived a cyclone in the Indian Ocean in April but made it to Port Louis, Mauritius, where it was overhauled and repaired.

In September, the *Jason* resumed its voyage, only to meet up with foul weather again, this time near Bermuda. The ship went on through numerous squalls and gales, passed Georges Shoal (about one hundred miles east of Cape Cod) and headed westward. This course, taken just after midday on December 5, "proved to be fatal as it was ill-advised,"

After ten months at sea, the British vessel *Jason* stranded near the Pamet River Station in Truro, where twenty-five men perished. One man, Samuel Evans, survived. *Cape Cod National Seashore.*

according to the U.S. Life-Saving Service report. Gale-force winds out of the northeast were increasing, and the early winter rain was quickly changing to snow and sleet.

By late afternoon, the Nauset and Cahoon Hollow Stations had already spotted the *Jason*, and the lifesavers up and down the beach of the Outer Cape began to prepare for the worst. According to the report, the *Jason* "was last seen by the day patrol, with upper topsails set, just off the three lights of Nauset, holding up to the windward with remarkable strength." Somehow, the vessel made it as far north as Pamet, but it was here where the surfman burned his Coston signal, followed by a report that the ship had indeed struck the bar. According to the Life-Saving Service report:

> *At about half past 7, Surfman Honey burst almost breathless into the station and exclaimed: "Hopkins* [the north patrol] *has just burned his signal." A moment later, Hopkins himself arrived and reported that the ship had struck.*

The crew of the *Jason* eventually "fled to the mizzen shrouds," and the ship lay with its starboard side to the waves, which the next instant lifted it farther shoreward and then fell crashing on board. According to the Life-Saving Service:

A few, more daring and desperate than the rest, still struggled to clear the boats. Another run of towering breakers was now about to leap on board, and the brave men were compelled to give over and quickly join their shipmates in the rigging. At this moment the red glare of the patrolman's signal gleamed through the darkness, and a cheer broke forth from the shipwrecked men.

However, their hope was short-lived, as high waves continued to pound the vessel. The captain was last seen standing on the ladder at the quarterdeck, supporting himself with a hand on each rail:

The mast toppled over, and eventually the crew members were washed overboard. Evans was swept shoreward, then back toward the rigging before being washed back to the beach, clutching the jute bale.

Once ashore, the young Englishman struggled to his feet and staggered toward Keeper Rich, who was carrying a lantern. He was taken to the station, wrapped in hot blankets and treated. The sixteen surfmen from the Pamet and Highland Stations were unable to find any other survivors.

Evans remained with the Life-Saving Service for several days and was believed to have stayed in Truro for a short time. He eventually was taken to the British Consul in Boston, which arranged for his transport back to England. Evans's father, William Evans, wrote to the Life-Saving Service, thanking the organization for its efforts and noting that "it is probable that he will again be sailing from England in February, I trust on a more favorable voyage."

Even though Evans somehow defied the odds on that fateful day aboard the *Jason*, his status as "sole survivor" would not last for long. In 1949, Cy Chase of North Eastham recalled for the *Cape Codder* that Evans's "sailing days came to an end" a few months after the *Jason* tragedy. "He fell out of a bunk and broke his neck."

Fortuna

Two Lost on the Back Shore

Although the three men had probably faced equally as great danger many times, something like a panic seemed to seize upon them, and a blind scramble for their lives ensued.
—U.S. Life-Saving Service Annual Report, 1894

During many of Cape Cod's historic shipwrecks, panic often overtakes the sailors on distressed vessels, making an already difficult situation much worse. That was the case of the fishing schooner *Fortuna* on February 12, 1894, when two men perished after the vessel ran aground off Race Point in Provincetown.

The *Fortuna*, which was launched only six months earlier, had left Gloucester earlier in the day and was off Highland Light. As nightfall approached, Captain John Greenlaw sensed that a snowstorm was coming, so he turned the schooner around and headed for Provincetown Harbor to ride out the gale.

Mother Nature had other ideas. By the time Greenlaw had retraced his course, snow and wind had picked up in intensity. "She was directly in front of the Race Point Lifesaving Station, but the captain still believed that he was to the westward of Race Point," according to the U.S. Life-Saving Service report. The sea broke heavily aboard the ship, and the anchor was dropped, sails were furled and torches were burned as signals for help. The red light of the Race Point lifesavers could be seen on Provincetown's back shore.

After a few more minutes, Greenlaw advised his crew of twenty-three men to "take to their dories at once and look out for themselves," the Life-Saving Service reported. "The dories were ten in number, stowed in nests of five; that is, one inside of another, one nest on each side of the deck amidships."

After a few more minutes, three dories were hoisted out. A fourth dory—with Abraham Brow, James McLain, Charles Anderson and Fred Lorenz aboard—was last. However, heavy surf lifted the fourth dory over the anchor stock, punching a hole in the side and filling it up with water. The Life-Saving Service reported:

> *Except for Lorenz, who was young and comparatively a green hand, all were strong men, with years of experience on the water. It might well have been expected that the entire number would get back on board without great difficulty, but such was no means the result.*

Greenlaw threw lines to all of them, and Anderson began to climb on board, with McLain clinging to Anderson and Brow holding on to McLain. Eventually, McLain and Brow were still left in the dory, and five other crew members tried, in vain, to pull them aboard. "Two or three times McLain was almost within in reach, and once one of the sailors actually got ahold of his oil jacket," the Life-Saving Service reported. A few minutes later, both McLain and Brow disappeared in the surf.

On land, Race Point keeper Samuel O. Fisher was already aware of the situation, shouting, "Vessel ashore!" to his men. The surfboat was quickly launched, but as the captain and the last two men were heading to shore in the dory, they were transferred over to the surfboat. Greenlaw assured the surfmen that no one was left on board the *Fortuna*.

Within an hour or two, all hands were accounted for on the beach. The *Fortuna* sailors were taken to the Race Point Station, while young Lorenz was cared for at the lighthouse. In the morning, all but the captain were taken to Provincetown, where they were provided with passes to the train and fed by the Seamen's Aid Society.

Had panic not overtaken them, McLain and Brow might have been among those heading home, the Life-Saving Service concluded:

> *Either could have been saved singly. But the combined strength of the five good men was not sufficient to draw up both at once; neither was McLain strong enough to hold to the rope with the weight of the frantic Brow added to his own.*

Smuggler

The "Hardest Rescue of All"

In one night, they had taken thirty-four men from two wrecks, and not a life lost!
—Donald Trayser, Provincetown Advocate, *July 30, 1942*

On the night of March 2, 1896, the crew of the Cahoon Hollow Station in Wellfleet had a visitor from out of town. This wasn't just any visitor, but a reporter from the *Boston Globe* newspaper, and he began to pepper Cahoon keeper Daniel Cole with all kinds of questions about the dangerous life of the surfmen. What was the most difficult rescue, the reporter wanted to know.

"The rescue of the *Smuggler* was the hardest of them all," replied Cole, referring to the transfer of all fifteen men from a stranded schooner during a storm just two months earlier. "The vessel struck at nearly low tide, which is the worst time, and when I saw the vessel with the crew in the rigging it did seem like a hopeless task for us, but our efforts were finally successful."

The night of December 30, 1895, was a busy one for the Cahoon crew. Earlier in the evening, nineteen men from the stranded vessel *Ellen Lincoln* were retrieved with (compared to other rescues) ease, but by 4:00 a.m., the *Smuggler*, out of Gloucester, had become stranded three miles south of the Cahoon Station.

Cole, fifty-one years old, was already a sixteen-year veteran as keeper. He was a longtime fisherman on the Cape and was a Civil War veteran, having accompanied General William Sherman on his "March to the Sea." Cole and his crew faced no easy task, using the horse-drawn cart to

Cahoon Hollow keeper Daniel Cole, *center*, referred to the rescue of the *Smuggler* as "being the hardest rescue of them all." *Cape Cod National Seashore.*

move the apparatus to the scene of the wreck. "The whirlwinds of sand sweeping along the shore blinded the men, and the horse at times refused to go," wrote J.W. Dalton in his 1902 book, *The Lifesavers of Cape Cod*.

In the July 30, 1942 edition of the *Provincetown Advocate*, historian Donald Trayser wrote that the *Smuggler* "rolled furiously" in the wild surf before the crew broke out the breeches buoy. On board the *Smuggler*, all fifteen men had climbed into the rigging while the vessel began to break apart. "Speedily the breeches buoy was hauled out, and hauled back again with the first sailor," Trayser noted. "Back and forth it was rushed, until fifteen men had been drawn from the rigging."

The lifesavers, it turned out, arrived just in the nick of time, saving the crew from what *Smuggler* captain Antone Courant said would have been "a watery grave." Trayser related the description of one of the crew members:

> *As the last man reached the surf line the masts of the schooner tottered and fell with a great crash. Her decks fell in a heap and only a mass of wreckage whirled about in the angry sea.*

Dalton recalled how the surfmen made it back to shore just in the nick of time:

> *The Lifesavers suffered terribly from the cold, and the rescue crew were nearly dead when they reached the shore. As the last man was pulled out of the surf, the vessel went to pieces, not a vestige being left to mark the spot where the disaster took place.*

The rescue also kept a perfect record intact. As of the night of the reporter's visit to Cahoon, "not a life has been lost off the coast within the district." Trayser marveled at the efficiency of the rescue:

> *The* Smuggler *was about three hundred yards from shore, yet in barely half an hour, fifteen men were hauled over and through the wild surf hat distance to safety. Loud were the praises, all alongshore, for Captain Cole and his crew.*

Bellmont

A Fifteen-Minute Disaster

Despite the celerity of the lifesavers, stranded vessels sometimes dissolve before the lifeboat can be got through the cordon of the surf and the inner bar breakers. Life has been lost as the result of the almost instant dissolution of the ship.
—New York Herald, *1911*

While the outer bars of Cape Cod claimed more than three thousand ships from 1626 through the mid-twentieth century, the men of the U.S. Life-Saving Service were able to rescue countless sailors from death. However, despite their heroic efforts, Mother Nature often proved to be too much of an adversary for the surfmen. Unfortunately for the barkentine *Bellmont*, only a few members of its crew were rescued after the 533-ton vessel, carrying a load of sugar from Cuba, crashed into the Peaked Hill sandbars on April 9, 1894. The *New York Herald* had this description of the disaster in a 1911 feature about the Life-Saving Service:

> [The *Bellmont*] *struck the outer bar during a howling, snow-laden gale and in a quarter of an hour, was rent into chips, not a vestige of her remaining in sight. She collapsed like a punctured balloon while the Peaked Hill boat was halfway between the shore surf and the inner bar, six of her crew perishing instantly.*

The *Bellmont* wasn't far from Boston when snow began falling on April 8, but the weather soon pushed it into the worst situation possible, according to the Life-Saving Service's annual report for 1894:

> *All hands became aware that they were just off Cape Cod, the most dangerous place on the New England coast during the prevalence of a northeast gale. The wind was heavy, the air thick with falling snow, and the sea running high. The only possibility of safety lay in speedily getting proper sail on the vessel and making a desperate effort to claw offshore.*

The vessel first struck the Peaked Hill Bars, about one thousand yards offshore, and was dragged to within six hundred yards of the beach, according to the Life-Saving Service:

> *A tremendous sea leaped on board over the taffrail, knocking off the cabin skylight and driving all hands, including the man at the wheel, into the mizzen rigging. Here, in less than fifteen minutes, she went totally to pieces.*

Keeper Isaac "Ike" Fisher and surfman Johnson looked over the predicament from the beach. Fisher "instantly realized that a dreadful disaster was at hand, and that only by the most expeditious and heroic work on the part of the lifesaving men could there be the least hope of deliverance for those on board the vessel, which he well knew was doomed to speedy destruction," the Life-Saving Service report said. Fisher, who had a hand in the rescue of 152 souls between 1880 and 1896, summoned assistance from Race Point and High Head, with Race Point providing the surfboat and apparatus, as the agency reported:

> *Knowing that in case of accident to his boat those who were in it would be carried to the westward,* [Fisher] *sent three of his crew up the beach in that direction, and with the four others boldly plunged the boat into the water and got safely afloat within five minutes from the moment the vessel stranded.*

The boat only made it about halfway to the *Bellmont* wreckage. "There goes the mizzen," one of the surfmen yelled, as the three masts spilled over. The Life-Saving Service reported that in three minutes, a piece of the deckhouse was the largest fragment visible:

> *There were three men upon this piece of wreckage, which now began to drift westward, and Keeper Fisher endeavored to reach it, but in doing so the wind and the sea were brought on the broadside of his boat, and they had to abandon the effort.*

Fisher and company retreated to shore and awaited the wreckage hitting the beach, but the Race Point crew, led by Keeper Samuel Fisher, had better luck, reaching the distressed men and pulling them ashore. Two of the shipwrecked men did not require emergency medical attention, but the ship's cook, John Stevens, was critically injured, the agency said:

> [Stevens had] *become tangled in the wreckage, where he nearly lost his life and whence he was rescued by the faithful and courageous efforts of his two surviving shipmates. When taken into the boat he was insensible, one of his arms was fractured in two places, several of his ribs were broken, one of his ears was nearly torn off, and his entire body covered with cuts and bruises.*

Stevens died the next morning, joining Captain W.R. Hagan and four other men, despite the surf crew's heroic efforts. "Not a single moment was lost nor the slightest error committed," the Life-Saving Service concluded. "Had she possessed sufficient strength to hold together barely ten or fifteen minutes longer, every man would have been saved."

Job H. Jackson Jr.

An Artistic Rescue

High above the howling of the wind and the roar of the surf sounded, occasionally, the voices of the apparently doomed men raised in chorus. It was a fearful scene.
—Barnstable Patriot, *January 12, 1895*

In late January 1895, Hannah Soule of Brockton, Massachusetts, bestowed an unusual gift on the crews of the Peaked Hill, Race Point and High Head Stations in Provincetown and Truro. Soule, a former resident of the Cape, "sent three large and handsome, framed, oil paintings as a gift…in recognition of their bravery in rescuing the crew of the schooner *Job H. Jackson Jr.* on January 5," according to the January 26, 1895 edition of the *Yarmouth Register*. "The paintings are sea pieces, wrecks and life-boats being the subject of each."

Eight men were rescued by surfboats from the *Jackson*, which struck the bars near the Peaked Hill Station during the early morning hours. Several attempts were made for a breeches buoy rescue, but the shots from the Lyle and Hunt guns fell short or missed their marks.

Peaked Hill surfman Levi Kelley was on his eastward patrol when, at 3:10 a.m., he "heard a snapping, rattling, and pounding of canvas" offshore, according to the January 12, 1895 edition of the *Barnstable Patriot*. Kelley attempted to light a Coston signal, but it malfunctioned, so he ran for the station. After running into fellow surfman William W. Cook, who was on the other patrol, they managed to get a Coston signal ignited and quickly managed to get everyone else out of bed and onto the beach while Captain Isaac Fisher phoned his colleagues at Race Point and High Head, according to the *Patriot*:

Peaked Hill Bars keeper Isaac Fisher, *center front*, and the crews of two other stations rescued the crew of the schooner *Job H. Jackson*. *Cape Cod National Seashore.*

> *A fierce wind of bitter, biting strength, carrying cutting sands on its pinions, swept pitilessly upon the workers, and soon from mustaches and beards hung great globules of congealed water, the frozen breath of working men. With faces and limbs nipped by the piercing cold they continued their humane work and prayed for dawn.*

Soon they were assisted by the High Head and Race Point crews, led by Captain Charles Kelley, "quiet but daring," and Captain Samuel O. Fisher, "whose courage has been put to the test frequently and always proved equal to the emergency," in the words of the *Patriot*. At dawn, the icy wreck of the *Jackson* was visible between the outer and inner bars, about six hundred yards from shore. The men of the crew, who took refuge in the warmth of the cabin but were soon flushed out by incoming sea water, were clinging to the rigging. As the *Patriot* noted:

> *Their craft was going to pieces, hull and rigging were covered by ice, making their clinging a thing of difficulty, and at any moment their frail mast might go by the board, carrying its precious human freight with it.*

Several shots by the Lyle and Hunt guns fell short, so Peaked Hill's Isaac Fisher, who was in command, opted for the surfboats. With an 11:00 a.m. low tide, the lifesavers waited until 10:00 a.m. for the rough water to subside. The *Patriot* praised the rescuers' efficiency:

> *On the beach, as orderly as if out on parade merely, the Lifesavers, three crews, worked with the quickness and accuracy of machines. All the varied assortment of guns, triangles, sand anchors and the full equipment for Lifesaving were ranged in apple-pie order right at hand.*

The captains selected their men. From Peaked Hill, it was Captain Isaac Fisher, Benjamin Henderson, William Wallace Cook, Charles Johnson and Edwin Whelden. High Head captain Charles Kelley chose Gideon Bowley, Fred Franzen, Seymour Holden, W. Hassenberg and Benjamin Kelley. The Race Point crew was Captain Samuel O. Fisher, Howard Hopkins, John Johnson, George Burch, George Bickers and James Kelley.

Race Point's boat, designed by surfman Bickers, set off on its maiden launch, followed by boats led by Captains Kelley and Sam Fisher. The Peaked Hill and High Head boats arrived at the wreck, while the other waited just inside the bar as a backup. The shivering men of the *Jackson* let out "a shout of joy" from the rigging and were soon on board the surfboats. "The journey to the beach was accomplished without mishap in lightning time and without a capsize on the shore landed," according to the *Patriot*. "Out upon the beach jumped the occupants, and one at least of the saved men fairly danced on the wet sand for joy."

Within the next few weeks, Soule's artwork arrived. "The donor sent three paintings," according to the *Register*. "One for each of the stations whose crews shared in the noble work of rescue."

Monte Tabor

Mutiny on the Back Shore?

More ghastly corpses never have been seen here.
—Boston Globe, *September 15, 1896*

On September 14, 1896, six Italian sailors lost their lives when the barkentine *Monte Tabor* stranded along the Peaked Hill Bars of Provincetown during a storm. Three of them died from being swept away by the high surf. The other three? They died by their own hands. Two men slashed their own throats, and the captain was found with a shotgun wound to the head.

The *Monte Tabor*, carrying a load of salt out of Genoa bound for Boston, was 155 feet long and 32 feet wide and had a burden of 592 tons. Just before midnight on September 14, surfman William Silvey of the Peaked Hill Station was on the east patrol and spotted a light a half mile from the station and close to shore. "High above the howl of the wind and roar of the surf could be heard the cries of the crew, as well as one single shot from some firearm," the *Boston Globe* reported on September 15, 1896.

The cabin boy saw the captain, first mate and another sailor disappear into the cabin. "Captain Luigi, who is said to have been temperate, kind, and brave, went laboriously among his men, kissed each one and said 'Saluta,'" the *Globe* reported. It was here that the three men took their own lives.

Surf conditions were too rough for a surfboat rescue, but before Peaked Hill keeper Isaac "Ike" Fisher and the lifesavers could do anything, the vessel was smashed to pieces by the high surf. The ship's clock washed ashore, having stopped at 12:20 a.m.

In this illustration from the September 15, 1896 edition of the *Boston Post*, six men were rescued from the barkentine *Monte Tabor*. *Author's collection.*

Three men were swept away by the waves and drowned. Six men held on to broken rigging and made it to shore. Another survivor washed up on the beach. "Craft struck in dark; see nothing, but all black, and big water come on us," said the one sailor who could manage a few English words. "We get in water, fall on timbers, and get flung way up on shore."

When the men got to shore, they spotted the lifesavers, but not realizing who they were, they feared for their lives. When they saw that the men were there to assist them, the sailors "hugged the knees of the station men and kissed them and seemed like men beside themselves," according to the September 15, 1896 edition of the *Boston Post.* At first, foul play was suspected, and the survivors were briefly jailed by the Provincetown sheriff before an investigation cleared the crew of any wrongdoing. "A report is current that a mutiny may have broken out on board, and the wrecking of the vessel was only a natural consequence," the *Post* reported on September 15.

It turned out that suicide was the only answer for an Italian captain whose ship failed to reach port, as was the case with the crew of an Italian bark off the coast of New Jersey a few years earlier. As the *Globe* noted:

> *It is an unwritten law among Italians that an army general should die on the battle field by an act of his own hand rather than live to acknowledge defeat, and that a commander of a vessel should go to the bottom of the sea with his ship rather than meet his fellow men and acknowledge his incapability as master. To the members of this race, to kill one's self is an act of bravery and not cowardice.*

The wreck of the *Monte Tabor* was one of the last rescues led by Fisher at Peaked Hill. He was transferred to the Wood End Station later that year. A total of 152 souls were "rescued from frightful peril," according to the *Globe*, by Fisher and his charges, an accomplishment that was acknowledged by the Massachusetts state legislature in a vote of thanks upon Fisher's transfer. "The recital of these few of the many valiant rescues wrought by gray-haired Isaac and his followers, is given simply that the public may know that the quiet and elderly man who takes command at Wood End Station is a hero tried and true," the legislature concluded.

Fisher requested a transfer to Wood End because he knew that the work there would be "better adapted to his declining years," according to the *Globe*. His superiors sympathized with Fisher, "who never shirked in time of danger." Fisher retired on May 31, 1901, after several weeks of being unable to fulfill his duties as keeper. He died on September 18, 1901, at the age of sixty-four and was buried at Hamilton Cemetery in Provincetown. His funeral was held at the Church of the Redeemer in Provincetown, with many Life-Saving Service keepers and officials in attendance. According to the *Globe*:

> *The floral offerings were many, among them being a lifeboat formed of white asters floating on a sea of roses and ferns, sent by the surfmen of the*

> *district, and a large breeches buoy crossed with an oar and boathook, resting on a bed of plans, sent by the keepers of the stations.*

In October 1901, Fisher was honored by King Hiram's Lodge in Provincetown. James Theriault noted in his book *Every First Monday* that the lodge adopted resolutions "describing his fearlessness in rescuing hundreds of shipwrecked seafarers and his marvelous dexterity with the steering oar."

Calvin B. Orcutt

Catalyst for a New Station

This unfortunate incident, in which eight lives were lost, was the catalyst in finally getting Old Harbor [Station] *built.*
—Cape Cod National Seashore's "Historic Furnishings Report: Old Harbor Lifesaving Station," 2005

In November 1977, the Old Harbor Station was hauled away from the eroding sands of North Chatham, moving the eighty-year-old structure to Provincetown and saving it from the encroaching surf. The station is now nestled on a dune top overlooking Race Point Beach, its memories and history intact. Its existence is owed largely in part to the wreck of the schooner *Calvin B. Orcutt* on December 23–24, 1896, according to the Cape Cod National Seashore:

> *An investigation by the assistant inspector of the First and Second Districts following the* Orcutt *incident concluded that the nine miles separating the Orleans and Chatham life saving stations was too great a distance for effectively preventing and assisting wrecks.*

The December 29, 1896 edition of the *Boston Globe* reported that "eight men were thrown to death in the merciless breakers." The nine-hundred-ton *Orcutt*, captained by L.H. Pearce of Manasquan, New Jersey, was caught up in stormy conditions near Pleasant Bay during the late afternoon hours of December 23. The December 29, 1896 edition of the *Chatham Monitor* reported:

> *Captain Pearce, evidently seeing no chance to work his vessel out of her perilous position, let go of his anchors with the hope of holding on and saving the schooner, but when she brought up she was right in the midst of the most dangerous breakers, which dashed over the ill-fated vessel, driving the men into the rigging, where they remained until 2 a.m.*

Pearce, thirty-eight, was described by the *Globe* as "one of the smartest men who ever trod a deck." His brother later commented that the captain often said, "My vessel shall never go on a lee shore with anchors on her bow." Pearce kept his word. "It cost him his life, however, for the anchors held her right over the bar, where she pounded to pieces."

Unfortunately for the crew of the *Orcutt*, the phone lines were down in the area, and by the time the surfmen from the Orleans Station, led by Keeper James Charles, arrived, a successful rescue had become highly unlikely. A

The Old Harbor Station in Chatham was constructed following the wreck of the *Calvin B. Orcutt* in December 1896. *Cape Cod National Seashore.*

breeches buoy line was shot from shore to the vessel, but the men on board were unable to take advantage of it.

Back in East Orleans, Benjamin Sparrow, District 2 supervisor for the U.S. Life-Saving Service, was alerted and headed to the beach to help out in any way possible. It was just one of many shipwrecks that he would attend to during a thirty-year career. "Word was sent in a roundabout way, telephone lines being down, to Superintendent Sparrow at Orleans, who footed it over five miles of beach, dune, and marsh to Orleans station," historian Donald Trayser wrote of the wreck in a 1946 edition of the *Cape Codder*.

"Sparrow was known for what we now call 'hands-on' management and was reported to have personally attended nearly every wreck that occurred in his district over a thirty-year period," according to Orleans historian Ron Petersen, who added that Sparrow was born in Orleans in 1839 and was often accompanied by his father, a volunteer lifesaver, to shipwrecks. A Civil War veteran, Sparrow was taken prisoner by the Confederates in 1862 before being released in an exchange.

The bodies of two sailors were found on the beach the next day, along with Pearce's overcoat and writing desk. "Anxious watchers, friends of the captain, the steward, and the engineer, who, with people from town to assist them, have day after day paced up and down the beach, watching for the cruel sea to give up the bodies of their dear ones," the *Globe* reported.

Besides the downed phone lines delaying any rescue attempts, the *Orcutt*'s dilemma was worsened by the relocation of a whistling buoy, located off Chatham, which drifted nearly a mile during a storm just one week earlier. "George Eldridge, hydrographer…believes that if the buoy had been replaced after it drifted December 16, the *Calvin B. Orcutt* would not have been wrecked on December 23," the *Globe* noted.

Funeral services were held a few days later at the town hall. The *Monitor* reported that the two recovered bodies were buried "in the public cemetery, only a few feet from the bluffs, where the surges send up their never ceasing dirge."

On February 1, 1897, the recommendation was made for construction of the new station, and construction was completed on February 18, 1898. The anchor from the *Orcutt* is now on display at Mystic Seaport in Mystic, Connecticut.

Catboat Tragedy of 1898

Just as the church bells in the town were calling the people to worship he died in my arms.
—Charles Hamer, Boston Herald, *October 1898*

When Charles Hamer of Harwich set out in his sixteen-foot catboat during the late morning of October 9, 1898, it didn't occur to him that it would be the last time he ever saw his two sons alive. Hamer, along with his boys, Joseph, nine, and Claude, eleven, and twenty-three-year-old Freeman Bassett, was sailing from Salt Water Pond in Harwichport to Stage Harbor in Chatham, but the journey ended with the boat capsizing, leading to the deaths of his two boys and Bassett.

While they were struggling to hold on to the overturned vessel, Joseph was carried away by a rough wave. Bassett died before dark. "The other little fellow, Claude, died in my arms about midnight," Hamer told the U.S. Life-Saving Service. "After the last link was broken, I sat in a stupor until daylight."

Conditions were pretty favorable after leaving port, but the vessel, sailing "with the boom swung well out to port," according to the Life-Saving Service report, capsized about one mile off Red River. Hamer told the Life-Saving Service:

> *As the wind kept hauling to the north, we soon carried it on the end of the boom, and as the boat sank in the trough of the sea the wind caught the sail*

> *on the other side, so that it became wrapped around the mast, and the peak halyards were thrown over the masthead.*

Hamer decided to move closer to shore, but Bassett had other ideas. Without notifying Hamer, Bassett climbed the mast and cleared the halyards. As reported by the Life-Saving Service:

> *The boat…immediately careened to leeward, the boom and sail dipping into the water and assisting to throw her on her beam ends. Bassett went over with the mast, while Hamer and the two boys were precipitated into the waves along the boat.*

Now hanging on to the boat, "Bassett seemed to become absolutely beside himself with fear," the report said. The boys were clinging to Bassett while Hamer tried to right the boat, but rough seas led to the trio's demise. Hamer told the *Boston Herald*:

> *While I was clearing the sail to get it away from the boat I saw to my horror that Bassett had gone crazy. I tried to pacify him, as the boat was still half full of water, and the slightest motion seemed to nearly tip her over.*

Claude grew weaker and his "courage gave out" before he died, Hamer said. Due to the boat being half submerged, spotting its dilemma from passing boats and nearly lifesaving stations was difficult. At 6:00 a.m. the following morning, Hamer's boat was seen by the Monomoy Station's lookout, and two surfmen headed out in a dory for the rescue.

The elder Hamer, sitting on a board with his feet in the water, was speechless and almost unconscious. According to the *Chatham Monitor*, Hamer "was nearly dead when rescued, being unable to speak, and his fingers clutched the side of the boat with a death grip, which made it almost impossible to remove him."

Hamer and two bodies were taken to the station. After one day, Hamer was returned to his Harwich home. Joseph Hamer's body wasn't found until three weeks later, by fishermen on the shore in Dennis. The catboat, found adrift near Chatham, was also recovered and returned to Hamer, who had praises for the surfmen:

> *I certainly think that the Lifesaving Service men did all they could. I am glad of this opportunity of reporting that fact, and testifying to their efficiency.*

Elsie M. Smith

"Perfectly Helpless"

Two of her crew of eighteen were washed into eternity without a moment's warning, after a brief but helpless struggle for life in the ice cold waters. It was a pitiful story of suffering and death which was told by those who escaped death.
—Yarmouth Register, *February 22, 1902*

During the early days of the twentieth century, shipwrecks were plenty along Cape Cod's Outer Beach. Many of these disasters saw the sailors panic and attempt ill-advised escapes before help could arrive. Such was the case of the Gloucester fishing schooner *Elsie M. Smith*, which struck the sandbars about 150 yards offshore between the Old Harbor and Orleans Stations just after 9:00 p.m. on February 13, 1902.

Two brothers, Dean Doucett and Silvina Doucett, were the casualties, but several other members of the crew were also among those who, ignoring their captain's orders, jumped into dories and tried to battle the raging surf trying to reach the beach. Others opted to climb into the ship's rigging.

Both D.N. Eldridge (of the Old Harbor station in Chatham) and M.K. Young (of the Orleans outpost), through the blinding snow, spotted the *Smith*, which was carrying ten thousand pounds of fish caught twenty miles offshore. Utilizing the nearby halfway house, they called their stations for aid.

As more lifesavers arrived on the scene, the fishermen who had attempted the escape by dory began washing ashore. One, James Rogers, "was too far gone to tell anything except that he and another man had jumped into a dory, and that the frail craft had capsized," according to the *Register*. Another, Fred Amiro, was "clinging to the craft with a deathlike grip" and was "more dead than alive." Louis Surett was another one who was recovered. He, too, was near death. According to the *Register*:

> *He said that he and* [the two brothers] *had jumped into a dory, hoping to be more successful than the others. They attempted to pull offshore over the bar, but had got only a short distance when a big comber capsized their craft, sending them all into the foamy billows, loaded with boots and oilskins, which they had hastily put on before jumping into the dory.*

The Life-Saving Service noted in its annual report:

> *They could not return to the vessel, and simply had to do their best to keep afloat and gain the shore a desperate chance, which only one succeeded in making good. The other two...were not able to contend successfully with the terrible odds, and in a few moments disappeared.*

The Gloucester fishing schooner *Elsie M. Smith* stranded between the Old Harbor and Orleans Lifesaving Stations on February 13, 1902. *Sturgis Library Archives.*

Surett found himself underneath the capsized dory and managed to work his way out of the oil jacket and boots—"how he did it he could not tell," the *Register* said. A half hour later, he was finally pulled to safety. Having noticed that Keepers Hezekiah Doane of Old Harbor and James Charles of Orleans were setting up the breeches buoy onshore, the crew opted to stay put on board the *Smith*, even though the vessel was showing signs of breaking up. *Smith* crew member William Akiman told the *Register*:

> *When we rushed on deck, the condition of things was simply awful. No language can describe it. We ran about like wild beings. What could we do? Some of us had on scarcely any clothing, and the freezing billows were breaking over the vessel fearfully. Every one of us thought our end had surely come, and we felt perfectly helpless. What more natural thing for us to do than throw out our dories and jump into them, hoping to be driven ashore in some way.*

A line was fired from the shore and hit its mark, and the remaining crew members were quickly shuffled to shore, the last one landing shortly after midnight. Akiman recalled:

> *Imagine our joy, therefore, if you can, when we found a line across our jibstay. We, of course, knew at once just what this meant, and we soon had it made fast. The Lifesavers worked like heroes, and we tried to take care of our end faithfully.*

The body of one of the brothers was recovered about one week later, near the Monomoy Lighthouse. Lightkeeper James Smith and his three daughters were notified of the washashore corpse. Emma Smith, the second daughter, recalled the incident for the August 21, 1904 edition of the *Boston Globe*:

> *I took hold of* [the body], *but I couldn't budge it, he was so heavy. Then father came, and we both took hold, and it groaned—from the stomach, you know; and blood started from the eyes and ears and mouth.*

Emma and her sister Annie, figured that the body, loaded with sand in the clothes, weighed more than three hundred pounds. His brother also came ashore, a little farther north near an area known as the "cut-through."

The vessel ended up being a total loss. Crew members were grateful that the death toll wasn't higher, but the Life-Saving Service concluded that those deaths could have been prevented:

> *Had the entire crew patiently remained on board the schooner until the arrival of the Lifesavers none would have been lost. On the other hand, had there been no Lifesaving stations in the vicinity, all as they themselves testify, must have frozen to death in the rigging, or, if they had drifted ashore, miserably perished on the bleak, midwinter sands.*

THE MONOMOY DISASTER

"WE MUST GO"

We must go. There is a distress flag in the rigging.
—Monomoy keeper Marshall Eldredge,
according to the U.S. Life-Saving Service Annual Report, *1902*

Cape Cod surfmen often did their jobs at the risk of losing their own lives—usually, there was no choice in the matter. But once in a great while, the lives of the surfmen were put in jeopardy when it wasn't absolutely necessary. Such was the case on March 17, 1902, after the coal barges *Wadena* and *Fitzpatrick* struck on Shovelful Shoal off Chatham during a northeaster. In an event that's come to be known as the "Monomoy Disaster," the rescue attempt of the *Wadena* claimed the lives of seven surfmen from the Monomoy Station. According to the U.S. Life-Saving Service report:

> *There was no more skillful or fearless crew on the whole coast, and since it appeared that the* Wadena *remained safe for days after the disaster, there was a general conviction that the men were practically a sacrifice, on the one hand to the needless apprehensions and senseless panic of the men from the barge, and on the other to their own high sense of duty, which not permit them to turn their backs upon a signal of distress.*

When the barges *Wadena* and *Fitzpatrick* were stranded in the shoals, owner William Mack came from Cleveland to help float the vessels. Mack chartered two tugs from Boston and hired four Portuguese workers from

Martha's Vineyard to shovel off the coal. "Coal towing is the least romantic and most dangerous business that is carried out at sea," wrote William Inglis in *Harper's Monthly Magazine* in 1907.

As the gale was starting, Mack sent his men to anchor near the shoals and, if it became rough, return to port. The *Fitzpatrick* stranded about a quarter of a mile south of Gull Point, with the *Wadena* settling about a quarter of a mile farther out at sea. The tugs headed to Hyannis to wait out the storm, while Mack and his men waited on board the *Wadena*. As Inglis noted:

> *So they ate their supper with good relish, smoked contentedly over their cards, and laughed at the foolish captains who had run away from no danger at all. All hands turned in at nine o'clock.*

Mack, however, was more concerned, and rightly so. By the morning of March 17, conditions had worsened. Shortly after breakfast, the *Wadena* had taken on three feet of water in the hold. Inglis wrote:

> *The sea was getting its clutch on the* Wadena. *If this pounding continued she must soon break up. Disconsolate, he went into the cabin, brought up an American flag, bent it on to the main rigging, union down, and raised it to the masthead. It was his acknowledgement of defeat by the forces of sea and gale. Whatever might happen to him and his Portuguese was in the hands of fate and the life-savers.*

Captain Marshall Eldredge of the Monomoy Station expressed surprise at the recklessness shown by Mack and his captain in staying on the barge, according to the *Boston Globe*. Eldredge walked four miles to the point to survey the situation and see if any bodies had washed ashore. Since the *Wadena* flew a distress signal, Eldredge and his six crew members were forced to attempt the ill-advised rescue. Eldrdege phoned in the news from the Life-Saving Service hut to Harwich Port's Seth Ellis at the Monomoy Station. Ellis and the Monomoy surfmen reached Eldredge, but in their haste they had made a costly error: they had forgotten their cork life belts. However, time was limited, so off they went.

After reaching the barge, Mack and his men were lowered into the surfboat, but panic overcame the Portuguese workers. "We are all lost!" one of them screamed. "Sit down you fool, or you will be lost!" Eldredge replied before turning to Ellis. "Seth, bat him on the head if ye have to, but git him down somehow."

Seth Ellis, *center front*, was promoted to keeper of the Monomoy Station in 1902 following the "Monomoy Disaster." *Cape Cod National Seashore.*

The panic continued, followed by a wave hitting the lifeboat, which capsized. The Portuguese men never surfaced, but the surfmen did and were soon back in the boat. However, more waves claimed the lifesavers one by one, until Ellis was the only one remaining.

Aboard the *Fitzpatrick*, Elmer Mayo and Ben Mallows witnessed the surfboat's distress, prompting Mayo to launch a dory. Despite the objections of Mallows, Mayo hurled the dory overboard and jumped in. By the time he reached the surfboat, Ellis had been stripped down to only shirt and pants and was nearly unconscious. Mayo was able to pull him aboard and row to shore. Mayo was taken to his house and Ellis to the lighthouse.

The other seven men of the Life-Saving Service perished: Keeper Eldredge of South Chatham; surfmen Isaac Thomas Foye of South Chatham and Arthur Rogers of North Harwich; and Osborn Chase, Elijah Kendrick, Edgar Small and Valentine D. Nickerson, all of Harwich.

One local resident, "Wicked" Walter Eldredge, could have easily ended up on that deadly rescue attempt. Prior to serving in the Life-Saving Service from 1904 to 1906, Eldredge worked substitute duty at the Monomoy Station. On the morning of March 16, he looked out his window and saw Elijah Kendrick

This page: The William Mack Memorial stands in front of the Chatham Lighthouse and Coast Guard station, recognizing those lost in the "Monomoy Disaster." *Author's collection.*

approaching. "There's Elijah, guess he wants me to sub for him," Eldredge recalled saying to his father in an interview for the April 11, 1946 edition of the *Cape Codder*. However, Kendrick kept going.

Mayo became known as the "Hero of Monomoy" and was awarded medals by the U.S. and Massachusetts Humane Society. He was offered the opportunity to go on exhibit as the hero of Monomoy for $100 per week, which he refused. His brother Ed jumped at the chance and "made a tidy sum of money," according to Inglis. Ellis was promoted to keeper of the Monomoy Station, where he served for the next five years. Both men were awarded Congressional gold medals. When the medals were presented, their bravery was lauded by the congressman in attendance. As Inglis recalled:

> *Elmer…looked long at Seth Ellis. A sudden sob broke the silence, and Elmer Mayo stumbled blindly from the platform with tears on his cheeks.*

A fundraiser in Boston, featuring both men, helped raise more than $36,000 for the families of those lost in the disaster. The service also authorized the construction of five homes in Harwich and Chatham for the widows and families.

Today, a tribute monument to Mayo, Ellis and those lost in the disaster stands at the Chatham Lighthouse. The U.S. Lighthouse Department authorized the construction of five homes in Harwich and one in Chatham—one for each widow and families of the six surfmen who lost their lives. One such home on Oak Street in Harwich Center was built for the widow of Edgar Small and is referred to as the "Monomoy Disaster House."

Onondaga

Freighter in the Sand

These were horse and cart days, and many Orleans residents plowed through the long stretch of beach sand with loads of the assorted cargo which were shipped away from the Orleans railroad station.
—Chatham Monitor, *January 14, 1937*

Whenever stories of giant ocean freighters being stuck on Cape Cod beaches surface, the first tale that comes to mind is that of the *Eldia*, which stranded on Nauset Beach in Orleans in March 1984. However, longtime Outer Cape beachcombers saw this movie long before 1984. The same thing happened on North Beach in Chatham, near the site of the Old Harbor Station in January 1907, when the freighter SS *Onondaga* stranded. And, oh, what a bounty it was.

The 2,696-ton *Onondaga* would be stuck in the sand for two months and, like the *Eldia*, became a wintertime attraction for many. The ship had a crew of twenty-eight, who were unharmed, but it was the $160,000 worth of cargo ($68,000 of it was damaged) that was being hauled off the ship—some legally, some illegally.

The two-year-old *Onondaga* left Boston on its usual trip at around 4:00 p.m. on January 12, bound for Charleston, South Carolina, and Jacksonville, Florida. After passing the lighthouses at Highland and Nauset, misty conditions took over, and before long, the vessel found itself in the shallows off Chatham, stuck in the sand. Two tugs and a revenue cutter tried to drag the ship away, to no avail. At this point, underwriters

The 2,696-ton freighter *Onondaga* sits in the sand on Nauset Beach after stranding there in January 1902. *Sturgis Library Archives.*

determined that it was time to unload the ship of its cargo, hoping that the lighter load would help the tugs' quest to tow the ship. It would take until March 14 before they were successful.

"Will the bones of the *Onondaga* bleach on Cape Cod sands?" the *Yarmouth Register* asked in its January 26, 1907 edition. "Almost every unemployed man in Chatham is given work bringing her cargo ashore," the *Hyannis Patriot* reported. "There is little hope that the liner, which is almost new, can be saved."

So began a long process of unloading the ship. According to a 1967 recap of the incident by the Chatham Historical Society's Joseph A. Nickerson in the *Chatham Shopper News*, the crew of North Chatham men who were called on to unload the vessel were J. Edson Jones, Rufus Nickerson, Norman J. Jones Jr., Arthur Griffin, George Nickerson, Frank Griffin, Alpheus Doane, Dexter Nickerson, Joseph A. Nickerson, William R. Speight and William Eugene Eldredge Jr. Nickerson noted that the cargo consisted of "everything from Dutch chocolate bars weighing over five pounds each, to smoked ox tongue, bolts of cloth, shoes, etc."

In his book *Mooncussers of Cape Cod*, Henry Kittredge wrote that among the cargo was "potatoes, mule hay, candy, gravestones, racing automobiles, whiskey, blankets, sheets, pianos, tons of wrapping paper, an organ, champagne, and coffee." Cases of candy and alcoholic beverages sat on the

The crew of the Old Harbor Station in Chatham poses in front of the beached *Onondaga* on Nauset Beach. *Sturgis Library Archives.*

A crew of Chatham men unload cargo—including Dutch chocolate, potatoes, whiskey and wrapping paper—from the *Onondaga*. *Sturgis Library Archives.*

beach, where locals helped themselves to these treats whenever they pleased. Nickerson told of a particularly odd haul of shoes from the ship:

> *One of our local men made his way home, after a hard struggle, with a case of shoes, only to find they were all left-hand shoes. It was in the mid-1930s that mother used the last of a bolt of "steamer cloth," a heavy oxford grey wool, to make herself a winter coat.*

On March 14, the *Onondaga* was freed and towed to Boston and then to Philadelphia for repairs. It returned to service, but a series of storms, strandings and collisions followed before the *Onondaga* sunk off the coast of Rhode Island in 1918. The bounty from the *Onondaga* on Chatham's shore wasn't forgotten anytime soon, as Kittredge noted in the recollections of Chatham's Clarendon Freeman, who told a friend:

> *I was shocked to observe the vandalism of my neighbors when I got to that steamer. There were men that I had known all my life, making off with whatever they could carry. Yes, I was shocked, and still more shocked to feel, before I had been there 10 minutes, an almost irresistible impulse coming over me to do the same thing!*

OAKLAND

DISASTER IN EARLY AUTUMN

As many mariners know, autumn can be a dangerous time on the high seas off Cape Cod. No one knew that better than those who observed the loss of the barge *Oakland* on October 13, 1913.

Two men were swallowed by the raging seas during a surprise storm off Highland Light in Truro, although they had an opportunity to be rescued. The *Oakland* and two other coal-laden barges were being towed by the tug *Paoli* from New Jersey to Boston. However, the storm picked up in intensity as the *Paoli* and its barges were preparing to round Race Point. The barges then separated from the tug, and the *Oakland* quickly dropped anchor about four hundred yards from shore. According to the October 15, 1913 edition of the *Boston Post*:

> *Captain Oliver wanted to take off the crew of the* Oakland, *but they refused the offer, believing that by anchoring they could ride out the gale in safety. Just before darkness set in the three men could be seen waving an American flag on a desperate attempt to attract attention. On the beach are the crews of the Highland Light and Pamet River Lifesaving stations waiting for the barge to strike. At present she lies just too far off shore for a line to reach her and the heavy sea makes it an impossibility to launch a boat.*

During the night, the *Oakland*'s anchors dragged, moving it closer to shore, giving the lifesavers hope that they would be able to fire a line to the vessel. Isaac M. Small, the keeper at Highland Light and author of the book

Shipwrecks on Cape Cod, kept watch over the distressed vessel, hoping that it wouldn't be crushed by the pounding surf:

> *We knew that a leak must sooner or later pour water into her hold. Soon we saw smoke rising from her pumping engine which indicated that water was coming in, and those on board were making an effort to prevent flooding of the hold, but we could see that they would be unable to overcome the leak and the water was slowly but surely sinking the craft.*

At this point, the two men aboard the *Oakland* attempted to row their dory to shore, Small wrote:

> *For about fifteen minutes they were able to keep the boat heading the sea, then came a great overpowering wave that swept the boat to its crest and sent it one hundred feet away, hurling the men into the rushing waves and turning the boat bottom up, for a brief moment the heads of the men appeared above the wild sea, then dropped from sight. Their bodies were recovered the next day far down the beach from where the sea swallowed them up.*

Several other vessels were claimed by the sea by the storm, including the barge *J.B. Thomas* off Wellfleet (four lives); the *Sumner H. Mood*, also off Wellfleet (all hands saved); the schooner *Henry D. May* off Chatham (all saved); and the *Henrietta A. Whitney* off Chatham, which was carried away.

As Small noted, you never can tell when it comes to autumnal conditions off the Outer Beach: "As an indication that the fine days of October sometimes turn to a wild tornado and terrific sea is shown in recalling the loss of the *Oakland*."

CASTAGNA

ICY END IN WELLFLEET

Coast Guard crews have seldom been called to such a battle as was theirs on that bitter winter morn of February 17, 1914.
—Henry Beston, "The Wardens of Cape Cod," for World's Work Magazine, *November 1923*

The surfmen of the U.S. Life-Saving Service and Coast Guard were known for putting their lives on the line every day. They came from all walks of life, and all ages were represented, officially and unofficially. One of the lifesavers who served in an "unofficial" capacity was none other than Eastham's Bernard "Bernie" Collins, the son of the Nauset Station's no. 1 surfman, Lewis Collins. He often accompanied his father to the seaside disasters, including the wreck of the *Castagna* on February 17, 1914.

The *Castagna*, an Italian bark carrying a load of guano, ran aground during a northeaster just south of the Marconi Wireless Station that morning. Heading for the Bradley Fertilizer Company in Weymouth from Montevideo, Uruguay, the crew of thirteen wasn't prepared for the rapid change in temperature. The *Castagna*, carrying a load of guano and cattle horns, crossed the Tropic of Cancer into the colder reaches of the Northern Hemisphere, where weather conditions offered up one winter storm after another. By the time the *Castagna* had reached the New England coast, it had been badly damaged, and several sailors had become ill and were losing the battle of keeping warm against the cold elements.

The *Castagna*, owned by Andrea Corrado of Genoa, Italy (his company has since grown into Gestion, one of the largest shipping companies in the world), was battered by repeated storms as it approached the Eastern Seaboard of the United States and found it increasingly difficult to sail north as it approached Boston.

Northerly winds prevented the vessel from navigating around the Outer Cape. Weary and chilled, the men were in no shape to fight for their lives when the ship struck the Wellfleet sandbar at 5:00 a.m. that morning, prompting Captain Giuseppe Garva to burn a white light. The Cahoon's Hollow surfman on patrol responded with a red Coston light, and a rescue mission was quickly under way. According to the Nauset Station's weather log, the temperature was fourteen degrees, with a stiff wind out of the north-northwest.

Unfortunately for the *Castagna* and its crew, the ship began to break apart, and as shipwrecked crews often did, the men climbed into the rigging. It proved to be a fatal mistake for many of them, including the captain. As Mate Luigi Oliveri told the *Boston Globe*:

> *Garva was right under me in the mizzen rigging. He was covered with ice and he became so cold that he fell and was knocked senseless and almost at the same moment a great wave swept him overboard.*

The surfman on patrol heard what sounded like gunshots coming from the vessel (it was actually the ship's jibs beginning to burst). The crews of the Nauset (Eastham) and Cahoon's Hollow (Wellfleet) Stations were summoned

Opposite: Two people observe the stranded Italian bark *Castagna* along Wellfleet's outer beach in February 1914. Five men perished in the icy wreck. *Sturgis Library Archives.*

Above: Abbott Walker, *center*, led the Nauset Station's rescue mission of the *Castagna*. He was Nauset's keeper from 1905 until his retirement in 1926. *M.J. Stevenson.*

to the scene just before 6:00 a.m. As Henry Beston wrote in his 1923 article "The Wardens of Cape Cod," for *World's Work Magazine*, the wreck was about four miles from each station—"four miles of northwest squalls, and deep, unbroken snow upon a wild, uneven waste."

The Nauset lifesavers were led by their keeper, Abbott Walker, who served in the Life-Saving Service and Coast Guard from 1896 to 1926. "I thought I'd go in for one year," Walker, who was the Nauset Station's keeper from 1905 until 1926, told the *Cape Codder* in 1947. "And I stayed 30." As a young man, Walker, born in 1864, worked as a fisherman in Wellfleet and a carpenter in Eastham. An old photograph of the Snow's baseball team in Orleans labels Walker as the local nine's shortstop. As a boy, Walker learned the art of handling boats in the surf, which served him well at the Orleans and Nauset Stations.

Walker replaced Alonzo Bearse as Nauset keeper in 1905 and retired to his South Eastham home in 1926. He died on November 29, 1954. Henry

Beston, author of *The Outermost House*, referred to him as "an expert among surfmen and boatmen, and one of the best liked and most respected men on all Cape Cod."

The Cahoon men were led by Keeper Edward Tobin, who moved up through the ranks at the Gurnet Station in Plymouth before taking charge in Wellfleet. During the rescue attempt of the *Castagna*, Tobin was rolled over under the surfboat and badly injured, nearly losing his life.

The crews had arrived by 7:00 a.m. Snow was petering out, but the wind and seas were still fierce. The tide was high, and gale-force winds were howling out of the northeast, creating high seas, so a surfboat rescue was out of the question for the time being. The lifesavers attempted to fire the breeches buoy on to the *Castagna*, but to the shock of the men on shore, no one on board was able to handle it.

As the tide lowered and the water receded, a surfboat finally made it out to the *Castagna*. Captain Garva and the ship's cabin boy were already gone, swept overboard by high waves before the lifesavers' arrival. Beston wrote in "Wardens of Cape Cod" that two men suddenly dropped "like ripe plums" into the sea. Eight men, suffering from severe frostbite, were rescued and taken to the nearby Marconi Wireless Station, where history was made twelve years earlier after Guglielmo Marconi succeeded in sending and receiving the first wireless messages between the United States and England.

Lewis and Bernie returned to the ship to search for more men, and what they found on board was horrifying. The first mate was hunched over the wheel box, with one hand frozen to the spoke. Bernie had to use an axe to cut away the spoke and free the man, who died shortly after reaching shore. Lewis then helped his son up into the rigging, where several members of the crew had retreated. The men were dead, covered in ice and frozen solid—Beston wrote that "their faces and bodies glassing over in strange mummy shrouds of ice." Bernie recalled a rather gruesome story for *Tales of Cape Cod* in a 1977 interview:

> [One] *man was—his arm was holding on to a piece of...like this, the arm was out there, and unfortunately the damn boat took a lurch, the ship rolled, and when she did, when I was lowering him down, he hit the deck with the arm sticking out, and that arm broke off just like a piece of glass. So we lowered him into the surf boat and then took his arm after him. And they took him, but he was frozen stiff. He wasn't alive. Deader'n a doornail.*

Heavy surf pounds the Italian bark *Castagna*. Surfmen from the Nauset and Cahoon's Hollow Stations combined to rescue a handful of men. *Richard Boonisar.*

After everyone was removed from the *Castagna*, the lifesavers entered the cabin, where they found a caged canary, still singing, and a gray cat "calmly waiting for them," as Beston noted in *The Outermost House*. The canary died shortly after its rescue, but the cat survived. Dubbed "Castagna" after the doomed vessel, the cat spent the rest of his days at the Marconi station. He would be one of many shipwrecked cats who found new homes on Cape Cod. "Go about in the cottages, and you may sit in a chair taken from one great wreck and at a table taken from another; the cat purring at your feet may be himself a rescued mariner," Beston wrote.

The *Boston Post* reported that "after a year and eight months, most of the time probably having been buried in the sand, [Garva's] body has come to light." It was discovered by Walter Moulton of Milton, Massachusetts, on Sandy Flats in Nauset Harbor near Orleans on October 15, 1915. "The captain's body was…washing out of the sands, still encased in ice," Orleans historian Al Snow wrote in the *Cape Codder* in 1966. "It had floated ashore, became buried in the sand and seaweed, and was well preserved."

The survivors were put on a train and taken to Carney Hospital in Boston. Some of them were forced to undergo amputations. They eventually returned to their homelands. Three of the bodies were buried in unmarked graves in Wellfleet.

One survivor of the *Castagna* shipwreck was a cat, soon named after the doomed vessel. He spent the rest of his days at the Marconi Wireless Station. *Cape Cod National Seashore.*

By the time Bernie was returned to shore, he was suffering from severe frostbite and was helped back to the Nauset Station. He was "packed in ice" and laid up for several days and felt the effects of that experience for the rest of his life. Bernie and his father later built the "Collins Cove" cottage colony on the shores of Town Cove near the Eastham/Orleans border. It's now a popular summer rental option for tourists.

As of 2020, the *Castagna*'s wheel was on exhibit at the Eastham Historical Society's 1869 Schoolhouse Museum. Bernie was asked to identify the ship's wheel several years after the incident and confirmed that it was indeed the same one he had freed the sailor from on that frigid morning in 1914.

The Canal

Cape Cod Forever Changed

On June 22, 1909, a project began that "would change Cape Cod forever," according to *Harper's Weekly*: the construction of the Cape Cod Canal, led by the efforts of New York financier August Belmont Jr. and his Boston, Cape Cod & New York Canal Company.

"Turning over the first spadeful of soil, Belmont said: 'I will never desert the task until the last shovelful is taken out,'" wrote Donald Trayser in the July 29, 1948 edition of the *Cape Codder*. "He secured William Barclay Parsons, a noted engineer and member of the Panama Canal Commission, to direct the work and the enterprise which had been envisioned from the time of William Bradford and the Pilgrims was brought to completion."

Eight vessels passed through the canal that day. The SS *Rose Standish*, with Belmont on board, was the first vessel to pass through the canal, which was only one hundred feet wide and twenty-five feet deep.

The privately owned toll canal, just over seventeen miles long, opened on a limited basis on July 29, 1914, and was completed in 1916. However, in 1915, toll revenues ended up being substantially less than investors would have liked, and several accidents didn't help matters. Belmont then attempted to sell the waterway to the government.

The canal was a project that was nearly three centuries in the making. The first formal proposal was made in 1697 but went nowhere with the Massachusetts General Court. Many more plans were submitted in the late 1700s and throughout the 1800s, all of which came up empty. There was a smaller canal on the Outer Cape, known as "Jeremiah's Gutter," which

August Belmont held a ceremony allowing the water from Buzzards Bay and Cape Cod Bay to meet, creating the Cape Cod Canal, on April 21, 1914. *Library of Congress.*

straddled the Orleans-Eastham border. Jeremiah's Gutter opened in 1717 and was used well into the 1800s but fell into disrepair.

Eyeing trade opportunities with the Dutch in what is now New York, Myles Standish and Governor William Bradford discussed the possibility of a canal on the Upper Cape during the 1620s. When Belmont and company began the canal project, Parsons and his team of engineers finalized the plans to connect the Manomet and Scusset Rivers. Even though Outer Cape shipwrecks were greatly reduced and nautical routes to New York were shortened by sixty-two miles, the construction was not without issues. Underwater boulders had to be blown up, and severe winter weather in 1910 slowed the project. Six workers died, their identities unknown.

On April 21, 1914, Belmont held a ceremony allowing the water from Buzzards Bay and Cape Cod Bay to meet.

The director general of the U.S. Railroad Administration took over jurisdiction and operation of the canal four days after the German U-boat shelling of a tugboat off Nauset Beach in Orleans in July 1918. The U.S. Army Corps of Engineers re-dredged the channel to 25 feet deep while it remained under government control until 1920. The canal remained under private ownership until 1928, when it was sold to the federal government for $11.4 million. After Franklin D. Roosevelt became president in 1933, New Deal funding of $4.4 million enabled construction of new bridges, which opened to traffic on June 21, 1935, and still stand today. The canal was eventually widened to 480 feet wide and dredged to 32 feet deep. It was listed as a National Historic Civil Engineering Landmark in 1985.

SHIPWRECK ON THE LINKS

Oh, we cut it in two, and ran it up on the cliff on skids.
—Isaac M. Small, as told to Arthur Wilson Tarbell,
Cape Cod Ahoy!, *1932*

Along the road to the Highland Lighthouse in North Truro stands a small cottage, with the name "*Coleraine*" in bold letters. Yet what really stands out here is the path that the cottage took to get here. "It is a very duck of an affair, quite unlike any other abode in the world," Arthur Wilson Tarbell wrote in his 1932 book, *Cape Cod Ahoy!* "It is the deckhouse of a barge, complete with pilot house, bridge, and steering wheel."

The *Coleraine* was one of three barges that stranded on the beach just below the lighthouse during a sudden spring snowstorm on April 4, 1915. The tugboat *Mars*, belonging to the Reading Railroad Company, left Bangor with the three barges a day earlier, heading to Philadelphia. When the weather suddenly worsened off Highland Light, the *Mars* captain cut the barges loose, leaving the crews of the *Coleraine*, the *Tunnel Ridge* and the *Manheim* to fend for themselves along Truro's outer bar. The raging storm surf drove the barges on to the beach, with the crews being rescued by the men at the Highland Station, just northwest of the light. The *Tunnel Ridge* and *Coleraine* were so badly smashed that they were not worth any attempt to float them, but the *Manheim* sustained only minimal damage.

Manheim's Captain George Israel and his men were rescued by the Highland crew's breeches buoy. "Captain Israel had mistaken the force of

The deckhouse of the *Coleraine* barge, wrecked in 1915, became part of the clubhouse at the Highland Links course in Truro. *Sturgis Library Archives.*

The barges *Coleraine*, *Tunnel Ridge* and *Manheim* after striking the beach near Highland Light in Truro in April 1915. *Sturgis Library Archives.*

This page: After the deckhouses were removed, the remains of the *Coleraine* barge were soaked with kerosene and burned on the beach. *Used with the permission of the Truro Historical Society.*

the sea on the outside off Cape Cod in a storm, and his barge dragging her anchors was forced nearer and nearer the shore," wrote Isaac M. Small in his 1928 book, *Shipwrecks on Cape Cod*.

The next morning, as the tide went out, the barges were on the beach. "One might walk dry-footed entirely around them," Small noted. Sand quickly built up around the *Coleraine* and *Tunnel Ridge*, and they had to be moved if the *Manheim* was to be floated. It was quickly determined that the best thing to do with the remains of the *Coleraine* and *Tunnel Ridge* was to burn them, so after kerosene was applied and torches lit, "the burning hulls lit up the sea and shore for many miles around," Small noted.

However, like so many times before along the Cape's shore, parts of this wreck found a second life. E. Hayes Small was told by Captain Israel that the locals could have the deckhouses of the *Coleraine* if they wanted them. After the houses were cut up into three pieces, the Truro folks undertook a massive moving project, as Small described:

> *Some planks were laid on the slope of the 100-feet high cliff, and with four horses the three parts were skidded to the top of the cliffs; then on trucks the parts were drawn to a point on the south side of the town road leading to Highland Light, there put together and converted to a three-room cottage. Later on, with a small addition on the south side, made the club house of the golf links.*

Captain Israel and two of his men lived on the *Manheim* until the following spring, making the necessary adjustments while waiting for suitable conditions to float the barge once again. On April 4, 1916, just one year to the day of the stranding, it was floated and able to engage in the coal transportation business again. As the *Barnstable Patriot* noted in the following weeks:

> *Barge* Manheim, *after lying on the beach near the Highland Coast Guard station nearly a year, and after repeated efforts upon the part of the Scott Wrecking Company, finally was floated last Saturday morning and towed to Boston by tugs* Neptune *and* Juno.

Thistlemore

"Imbedded in the Sands"

"The Wreck of the Thistlemore" by Ross Moffett is dramatic in spirit, and through the ship itself is no more than a gray shadow on the horizon, the artist has given us a more interesting picture of the event by centering his emphasis on a black horse that pulls the lifeboat toward the shore.
—art critique of an oil painting, Helen Comstock, Arts and Archaeology Magazine, *January–June 1922*

For many years, Cape Cod shipwrecks provided a source of inspiration for the peninsula's artists. Provincetown artist Ross Moffett was one such painter and captured the dark and somber spirit of the stranding of the steamer *Thistlemore* along Provincetown's back shore on February 7, 1922.

Ships were often caught up in the notorious currents near Provincetown's Race Point, and the *Thistlemore* was no different during a storm-force snow squall that night. When the vessel suddenly crashed into the outer bar one mile north of the Peaked Hill Bars Station, the crews of Peaked Hill and Race Point quickly departed their respective dinner tables and were on their way to the rescue.

Leading the way for the Peaked Hill crew was Emanuel Gracie, who was promoted to the commanding officer post in 1921. Gracie grew up in Provincetown and had previously served for two years at Peaked Hill from 1915 to 1917. Gracie and his men, complete with apparatus, were soon on the scene, about to embark on "a pretty strenuous night of it," according to the February 13, 1922 edition of the *Barnstable Patriot*:

> *The terrific sea which the ever-increasing northeast gale had kicked up, the darkness and the distance from shore of the stranded ship made any attempt to launch a life boat foolhardy and a mortar line could not reach her. The only thing to do was to await daylight, signal fires were kept burning on the beach to encourage those on the ship.*

According to the February 8, 1922 edition of the *New York Times*, the Coast Guard cutter *Tampa* had arrived during the evening hours but was unable to offer assistance. The *Thistlemore*, heading from Boston to New York carrying a crew of forty-four men, was still outside the bar as dawn broke on February 8. The vessel first struck at high tide the night before, and another high tide was certain to drive it over the bar. By 8:00 a.m., the rising sea had done just that, and "the vessel was solidly imbedded in the sands and in no immediate danger," according to the *Times*. A line was shot to the ship, setting up the breeches buoy.

Captain Emanuel Gracie, keeper of the Peaked Hill Bars Coast Guard Station, leads the breeches buoy rescue of eighteen men from the freighter *Thistlemore*. *Leo Gracie.*

By 9:30 a.m., the first man was being brought ashore. By noon, most of the *Thistlemore*'s crew was ashore. As winds moderated, Captain Fortune and a few members of his crew decided to stay on board. The following week, the *Boston Globe* reported that the *Thistlemore*'s "bottom plates were completely damaged, and the engines were forced out of alignment." Later that week, the 4,146-ton *Thistlemore* was floated by tugs at high tide and towed to Boston for repairs.

Gracie, who died in 1946 at the age of sixty, would go on to win "wide praise for his exploits in Coast Guard service," according to the *Provincetown Advocate*. While the *Thistlemore* wreck was considered dark and somber both in person and on Moffett's canvas, Gracie would be involved in even more tragic rescue missions over the next few years.

Annie L. Spindler

Wreck of a Rumrunner

The captain had shown the Coast Guard that his papers were in order [he was ostensibly bound for the West Indies] *and had demanded protection for his cargo.*
—Cape Cod Way, *1955*

During the Prohibition era from 1920 to 1933, when a rumrunning vessel ran aground on the beach right in front of a Coast Guard station, it was a pretty good bet that the boat and its crew would be out of business for a very long time, if not forever. But in the case of the schooner *Annie L. Spindler*, which ran aground near the Race Point Coast Guard Station in December 1922, the skipper somehow managed to get a good deal of his hooch back.

The vessel, built in 1910 as a fishing boat in Nova Scotia, was carrying somewhere between six hundred and eight hundred cases of whiskey, depending on the reports. After the crew "was trussed to the rigging in a storm of almost hurricane strength for hours," according to the January 1, 1923 edition of the *Barnstable Patriot*, the two-masted vessel struck at Race Point, only ten minutes after being spotted by the surfmen of the Race Point Station. The crew was rescued by breeches buoy and cared for at the station. Following the rescue, the illegal cargo was discovered, but the *Spindler*'s skipper was ready. "Her papers showed that she was bound from St. Pierre/ Miquelon to Nassau," according to a report in the *New York Times*.

The rumrunning schooner *Annie L. Spindler* ran aground at Race Point Beach in Provincetown. After having his cargo confiscated, the captain managed to get most of it back. *Sturgis Library Archives.*

Race Point keeper Irving Collins wasn't taken in, but he had no choice but to store the booze away at his station. At this point, several cases of whiskey had already disappeared from the ship, as the locals managed to carry it away before the Coast Guard could get at it. Coast Guard trucks then hauled the rest of the booze to a harbor wharf, where a second vessel, "also outfitted with papers made out for the West Indies," according to *Cape Cod Way*, picked it up. Once they were in the clear, the liquor was dropped off, without issue, at a beach across the bay in Plymouth. After the local wreckers cashed in on some of the alcoholic treasures washing ashore, the beach was still full of onlookers, watching the surf, driven by a bitter north wind, bash the boat to pieces.

Thanks to his clever work with the ship's papers, the skipper managed to salvage most of his haul. Countless rumrunners—many of whom did their business with Canadian, European and Caribbean ships anchored in "Rum Row," twelve miles offshore—weren't so lucky. Being caught by the Coast Guard usually meant a $10,000 fine, and the offending vessel was confiscated by the government.

The Prohibition era began in 1920 following the passage of the Eighteenth Amendment, but it was later repealed with the passage of the Twenty-First Amendment in 1933. Cape Cod, with its abundance of estuaries and deserted beaches, was a landing ground for many rumrunning vessels. The liquor was then loaded onto cars and trucks and transported to the big cities, such as Providence, Boston and New York. Many a Cape Codder prospered from boats, on the run from the Coast Guard, that dumped their cargo overboard.

And what of the wreck of the *Annie L. Spindler*? Well, it's gone now, swept away by the waves, but the wreckage, according to *Cape Cod Way*, "became quite famous as a place where young couples came at night to spoon in solitude but seldom succeeded because the deck was usually packed with other couples similarly inclined."

The *Emerald* Fire and the One-Hundred-Mile Journey Home

The crew told many tales of "hardships they endured while battling the flames with buckets of water and while making desperate efforts to reach land through miles and miles of rough seas."
—Boston Post, *March 27, 1925*

The history of Cape Cod is filled with many stories of ships running aground, but there were also several instances where another hazard endangered lives—namely, fire at sea. That's what the crew of the fishing schooner *Emerald* encountered about one hundred miles east of the Cape on March 26, 1925, when the vessel caught fire and forced the crew of twenty-six men to abandon ship. Fortunately for the crew, they were able to escape by way of seven dories and eventually make their way back to shore.

The *Emerald* burned to the water's edge and then sank. "The flames raced from stem to stern and when the situation became hopeless the dories were put over and the men, with what little food could be saved, pulled away," reported the *Boston Post* the following day. The fire began following an explosion just before 10:00 a.m. "The only explanation is that leaking gasoline used for generating the electric light current, ignited," according to the *Post*.

Over the twenty-four hours after the fire, Captain Lawrence Norris and his men, several of whom were from the Cape, headed west in their boats. The men landed at various stations along the Cape's Outer Beach, including Highland Light (a group that included John Souza and Domingo Josephs of

Provincetown), Race Point (John D. Silva of Provincetown was in this boat), Pamet River and Peaked Hill. Norris and John Lisbon of Provincetown were among those who landed on the shore of the Cape tip town. Most of the other men were from the Boston area.

The Highland boat of survivors caused "considerable excitement" in Truro, as reported by the *Yarmouth Register*. The men were rescued by Keeper Anthony Tarvis and his Coast Guard crew, who spotted them three miles out at sea. The *Register* later reported that a "Miss Williams from the Marine Station at Highland Light drove down to the beach [and] got the story from the shipwrecked men for the Boston papers." The *Post* said that "upon arrival, the men were exhausted and could give only a few details."

The landing for crew members George White, Lewis Dunn, Michael Fay and John Tabaca in Provincetown was particularly difficult. The quartet became separated from the rest of the crew on their trip toward shore and, according to the *Post*, "were thrown into the water a few hundred yards from Provincetown beach when the heavy surf capsized their small craft. By clinging desperately to their overturned boat the men saved their own lives, the heavy seas having floated the small [craft] in shore with the tide." The men were later sent to Boston's South Station from Provincetown by train. As the *Post* reported, "Dressed in their fishing clothes, all that was left of their personal belongings, the survivors were met by scores of anxious friends and relatives."

USS *Morrill*

Rum Chaser on a Rampage

The cutter known as the USS *Morrill* had already seen a tough stretch of luck as the day dawned over Provincetown Harbor on November 16, 1926. The *Morrill*, known as the "mother ship" of the rum-chasing fleet along the New England coast during the Prohibition era, had seen eight of its men perish as one of its surfboats capsized off the coast of Nova Scotia one year earlier, but what was to come later on this day defied explanation.

The *Morrill*, which was fitted with machine guns and had captured a British schooner transporting more than 2,500 cases of alcoholic beverages off Highland Light just a few months earlier, was anchored in the harbor as winds began to pick up steadily out of the southeast during the day. By late afternoon, wind speeds reached gale force, increasing the waves battering up against the vessel. By nightfall, the winds were up to hurricane force, forcing the chains and anchors to snap.

The three-hundred-foot vessel was on the loose, drifting about helplessly and headed for the docks of the harbor. The fifty-man crew could do little to stop it, except to issue a warning via megaphone to those onshore to get off the wharves and out of the buildings.

"Swinging to the right she crashed into a fishing boat and sent it to the bottom, then sharply to the left she sent another fishing boat to destruction, continuing her swinging, zigzag course until she had passed over or through three more boats," was the description written by Isaac M. Small in his book *Shipwrecks on Cape Cod*.

The boats were only the beginning of the *Morrill*'s unintended path of destruction. According to the *Provincetown Advocate* from that week in 1926, the *Morrill* "drifted in between Higgins' Wharf and Pickert's Canning Factory Wharf and with the tossing about both wharves were completely demolished. The bow of the big boat struck one wharf and the stern the other wharf."

The Casino, a restaurant/nightclub that was closed for the season, and a fish market were among the physical casualties of the *Morrill*'s rampage, as well as "a new garage aboard Higgins' Wharf [that was] thrown upon the tide and washed ashore," according to the *Advocate*:

> *She drifted in between Higgins' wharf and Pickert's Canning Factory wharf and with the tossing about both wharves were completely demolished. The bow of the big boat struck one wharf and the stern the other wharf.*

After the *Morrill* hit the wharves, "her further progress was then checked but not until she had landed within a hundred yards of the main street in Provincetown," according to Small. Storm damage was also extensive, as the beach area was "littered with what logs and debris by the ton." The disaster brought throngs of people to the harbor, according to the *Advocate*:

> *The street was lined with hundreds of sight seers who were horrified at the destruction, the crashing and smashing of timbers. The vicinity looked like the aftermath of the Florida hurricane with the great amount of debris.*

Amazingly enough, there were no fatalities or injuries. Within the next few days, the *Morrill* was freed from the shoreline by a pair of Coast Guard destroyers, the *Acushnet* and the *Ossipee*, and pulled into deeper water. From there, it managed to make the trip to Boston for repairs. The *Morrill*, first commissioned in 1889, didn't stay on the high seas for long after that, as it was decommissioned in 1928. As far as the damage, Congress acted on a measure in 1927. According to the *Barnstable Patriot*:

> *In the first deficiency appropriation measure passed by the House, provision is made for the settlement of claims for damages under $1,000 caused by the running aground of the Coast Guard cutter* Morrill *at Provincetown.*

MONTCLAIR

LIFESAVERS SHORT-HANDED

There has just been a great wreck, the fifth this winter and the worst. On Monday morning last, shortly after five o'clock, the big three-masted schooner Montclair *stranded at Orleans and went to pieces in an hour, drowning five of her crew.*
—*Henry Beston,* The Outermost House

The list of wrecks along the Outer Beach of Cape Cod is a lengthy one, with several tragedies registered during the winter of 1926–27. One of the most memorable disasters of that season occurred on March 5, 1927, with the wreck of the *Montclair* along Nauset Beach in Orleans.

The Coast Guard turned in yet another heroic effort, as two members of the Canadian vessel's crew were rescued by the crew at the Orleans Coast Guard Station. The problem was that only Keeper Edward Clark and two surfmen, Wilbur Chase and John Adams, were on duty that fateful morning at the Orleans station, which was in the process of being shut down. The neighboring Nauset and Old Harbor Stations, meanwhile, still had three times as many men on call.

Unfortunately for the crew of the *Montclair*, which left Nova Scotia three days earlier and was bound for New York with a load of twenty-five thousand bundles of laths, it ran into a northeaster and found itself in trouble on the outer bars of Orleans.

"Sometimes the government has fits of economy, but the Coast Guard service is a poor place to begin the practice of it," wrote Isaac Small in

The schooner *Montclair* was wrecked during a storm near the Orleans Coast Guard Station in 1927. Five men died, while two survived. *Eastham Historical Society.*

his 1928 book, *Shipwrecks on Cape Cod*. "Had this station been manned it is quite probable that every man of the crew of this craft would have been saved."

Clark, a twenty-five-year veteran of the Coast Guard/Life-Saving Service, woke in the predawn hours to the howling of the wind. He spotted the schooner pounding on a sandbar about one mile offshore and summoned Chase and Adams, both twenty-year veterans. The three-man crew, which managed to enlist the aid of a few local volunteers, attempted to launch the surfboat but didn't get far.

Clark knew that he and his crew needed help, but another problem presented itself. The phone lines were down, cutting off communication with the neighboring Coast Guard stations in Eastham and Chatham. One volunteer walked five miles to the Old Harbor Station in Chatham and the other four miles to a telephone in Orleans to call the Nauset Station. The details were rushed to Orleans via automobile.

Unfortunately for the crew of the *Montclair*, time was running short. The front end had broken apart, and Captain William McLeod ordered the crew to set up safety lines along the rear deck and stay there. Armed with the breeches buoy, the Coast Guards shot two lines over the stern. Five crew members, including McLeod, held on to the first line, and two other sailors, Garland Short and Nathan Baggs, grasped the second line. A large wave

Wilbur Chase was one of only three men on duty at the Orleans Coast Guard Station when the *Montclair* stranded in 1927. *Mary McDermott.*

then came crashing in and swept the five men on the first line into the ocean. Short and Baggs managed to hold on and were pulled ashore.

It wasn't long before McLeod's body was recovered from the surf about six hundred yards south of wreck. When the captain's body was being carried into the Coast Guard station, Short and Baggs became hysterical, insisting that they assist with the rescue effort. The men were restrained and were treated by Dr. H.D. Handy of Harwich. The next day, the Coast Guards found two more bodies, two miles down the beach. The last victim was found by a beach walker five miles to the south one week later.

Clark took the loss of life hard. "He has an enviable reputation in the Coast Guard service," the March 6, 1927 edition the *Boston Globe* reported. "Just a quarter of a century ago he signed up for service and had always saved those he went after until today."

As Henry Beston noted in his book *The Outermost House*, "There he saw ahead of him a hand thrust up out of the great sands. Beneath he found the buried body of one of the *Montclair*'s crew."

A full crew went back on duty in Orleans on December 1, 1927, but as Small noted, "This seems to be another case of locking the stable door after the horse has been stolen."

During the summer of 1962, Baggs, living in Dartmouth, Nova Scotia, was glancing at the latest edition of *National Geographic* when he came across a lengthy feature on Cape Cod. Flipping through the pages, the sixty-six-year-old retired sea captain came across a photograph that took him back forty-one years. The photograph was of young children frolicking about on a sunny day across the sands of Nauset Beach in Orleans. One of the kids was jumping off the skeletal remains of the *Montclair*.

Baggs vowed to return to the scene of the wreck someday, and six years later, he did just that. On September 10, 1968, he returned to the scene. Described by the *Cape Cod Times* as "medium height, spare of build, with a rugged countenance, and soft spoken," Baggs arrived with his niece and her husband on a Saturday afternoon. Rainy weather kept them from venturing any farther, but three days later, they returned and finally reached the site of the wreck. One of the people he met on the beach was Norman Hopkins, who along with Willis Gould, Alfred Hopkins, Fred Avataggio and Bruce Mitchell were a group of local volunteers who had pulled Baggs and Garland Short from the water on that fateful day. Baggs sat down on the wreck and recalled the wreck's events to the *Times*:

> *It was rough...we were just lying there hanging on. They kept trying to get a shot line to us. The tide moved us closer and we finally got a line aboard. I tied Short to the line, then myself, and we jumped overboard.*

Baggs returned to Nova Scotia and worked as a sea captain for Imperial Oil for forty years before retiring. Short worked at a shipyard in Halifax. Baggs recalled meeting up with Short at a Masonic Lodge meeting in 1966. While reminiscing about the *Montclair* disaster on the sands of Nauset Beach, Baggs recalled the valiant efforts of his rescuers and wished that he had stayed on Cape Cod. "They were very good to us," he told the *Times*. "As a matter of fact, they wanted me to join the Coast Guard. I'm sorry now that I didn't."

CG-238

A Premonition of Disaster

Muffle your drums, O sons of the sea.
Let decks in silence stay;
For comrades' souls have passed from thee.
And mates have died this day.
—Ensign E.W. Holtz, USS Vaughan, *Coast Guard vessel of San Pedro, California, "Sons of the Sea," published in the* Boston Globe, *1927*

In February 1927, the Coast Guard career of Jesse Rivenback was looking up. He had just been transferred from the New London base and was promoted from chief boatswain's mate to boatswain. The former merchant marine officer, thirty-six, was married and living in Oaks Bluff on Martha's Vineyard.

And yet Rivenback had a deep sense that darkness was on the horizon. His upcoming tour of duty, on patrol on the *CG-238* for the "Rum Tour," was to go around Cape Cod and head to Boston. He was feeling more than a little uneasy. This was a premonition of impending disaster. "You know, I don't feel right," Rivenback told a friend. "If anything should happen, have my body sent to Wilmington [North Carolina]."

It proved to be a bad omen. On February 20, Rivenback and his eight crewmen were lost at sea off Cape Cod in a storm that many regarded as the worst since the "Portland Gale" of 1898. The crew members are now listed on the National Law Enforcement Officers Memorial in Washington, D.C. Only the bodies of two victims—Raymond Clark and Charles Freeborn—were recovered, with Clark's watch stopped at five o'clock.

The *CG-238*, one of many seventy-five-foot cutters utilized by the Coast Guard during the Prohibition era, found itself plagued by engine trouble as it approached Boston on the night of February 19. The boat was then cast seaward, and the anchors, dragging for a time, eventually let go. Keeper E.B. Andrews and his crew at the Highland Coast Guard Station in Truro picked up a message by way of "the blinker" of "anchors dragging," but increased intensity of the storm prevented further communication throughout the night. The Coast Guards could still make out a flicker or two of the boat's light but could only watch helplessly, as the vessel was too far from shore to attempt a breeches buoy or boat rescue.

The CGs were able to make out another blinker message that the vessel was in a dire situation. A high tide was expected at about 3:00 a.m., and the CG station signaled to the boat to weigh anchor in the hope that the tide might carry the boat over the outer bars and on to the beach. "If the tide had done this, the men, in all probability, would have been saved," according to an Associated Press report.

Two destroyers from Boston were summoned, but due to their own issues in the face of hurricane-force winds, they fell just short of reaching the doomed cutter. As the *Boston Globe* reported, "One mighty engulfing wave swept the boat to destruction, and the crew to a death the merciful suddenness of which was possibly more welcome than the agony of waiting."

It wasn't long before the CG-238 went to pieces, with most of it being swallowed up in the sands of the outer bar. Several fragments of the boat were found on the beach, but a squad of twenty-five men was unable to find Rivenback and the other members of the crew.

As Isaac M. Small wrote in his book *Shipwrecks on Cape Cod*, "Frequently from the distressed boat came frantic cries across the surging waters, but no earthly power could reach them."

S-4 Submarine

Forty Men Trapped

Provincetown, long hardened to wrecks, now witnessed horror such as she had never known before. Slow suffocation within steel walls, one hundred ten feet below the surface, went on for days, while divers struggled to save the men with whom they could exchange messages by tapping in international code.
—Joe Berger (aka Jeremiah Digges)

While shipwrecks along Cape Cod's Outer Beach numbered in the thousands, the number of submarine setbacks was far less. Two come to mind: the 1925 stranding of the *S-19* in Nauset Harbor and the sinking of the *S-4* submarine just off Long Point in Provincetown on December 17, 1927.

The *S-19* was spared any fatalities, but the *S-4* disaster, following a collision with the Coast Guard destroyer SS *Paulding*, resulted in forty deaths due to carbon dioxide poisoning on the floor of Provincetown Harbor. The December 22, 1928 edition of the *Yarmouth Register* described the 3:37 p.m. collision:

> [The *S-19*] *was making her last submerged run of the day and was rising to the surface off Wood End Light when she was rammed by the Coast Guard destroyer* Paulding *which was on rum patrol and which was running into Provincetown Harbor to look over some sailing craft anchored there.*

Storm warnings were also up, as high northwest winds were gusting over Cape Cod Bay. The *Paulding* found nothing in the way of rumrunners, as the liquor smugglers rarely braved stormy conditions. The *S-4*'s periscopes were slightly exposed but "would have been clearly visible to any alert observer aboard the destroyer," according to historian Joe Berger's account in the *Provincetown Advocate.*

Boatswain Emanuel Gracie, coming up to the observation room, asked Frank Simonds of the Wood End Station what he saw offshore. "Not much" was his reply. "But there was a submarine on the test run not long ago." Gracie looked through the telescope, and near the end of the measured mile, he saw the periscopes. "Good God, there's going to be a collision!" Gracie yelled.

The *Paulding* rammed the *S-4*, punching two holes in a ballast tank and another in a pressure hull. The sub was quickly flooded with freezing water and began to sink. The *Paulding*'s crew immediately marked their position and radioed their superiors while Gracie prepared a lifeboat for launching.

According to the Submarine Force Museum of Groton, Connecticut, thirty-four of the forty men on board were alive in the control room, the engine room and the motor room. Only six men who had been stationed in the torpedo room were unaccounted for, but the situation began to deteriorate quickly.

The Coast Guard summoned the salvage ship *Falcon* from New London, Connecticut, and divers from Newport, Rhode Island. Pontoons were sent by tug from New York. The *S-4* was struck at 3:37 p.m., but the *Falcon* didn't arrive until 7:00 a.m. the next morning. Diver Tom Eadie descended and caught an answering signal from the torpedo room—six taps, indicating that six men were still alive. When Eadie checked on the thirty-four men in the engine and motor rooms, there was silence, indicating that they had not survived.

On December 18, a second diver, Fred Michels, attempted to connect a tube to the *S-4* and pump in fresh air, but weather conditions were still unfavorable. Michels then reported that his own air line was fouled. According to the Submarine Force Museum:

> *Eadie, still exhausted from his first dive, went down again to save his friend but could not find the air hose that was supposed to be attached to the sub. With the weather growing worse,* Falcon *turned for Boston with the nearly-dead Michels within her decompression chamber. He would survive and Eadie would be awarded the Medal of Honor for saving his life.*

A monument to the forty men lost in the *S-4* submarine tragedy now stands on the property of St. Mary's of the Harbor Church in Provincetown. *Author's collection.*

Another attempt to connect the air tube was made, but it was too late. There was no answer, and the analysis of the carbon dioxide levels in the submarine indicated they were far too high for anyone to survive.

Three months later, the sub was finally raised and towed to the Charlestown Navy Yard in Boston. A naval court of inquiry blamed the commanders of the colliding craft and Rear Admiral Frank Brumby, who was in charge of the rescue operation, but the secretary of the navy overrode the decision, leaving the deceased commander of the *S-4* with the full responsibility.

The ordeal left the families of the lost crew members devastated, while the people of the Outer Cape were also left wondering about the efficiency of their government. Berger "graphically and often with ill concealed disgust" opined in the *Provincetown Advocate*:

> *Provincetown was tense, spoke in whispers and walked slowly, almost on tip-toe, during those anxious moments following the sinking of the* S-4. *Fishermen and their folk, eager to do all in their power to save the forty men trapped in the submarine, railed at the inaction and stupidity of Washington.*

A cross from the *S-4* now stands in the garden of the Church of St. Mary of the Harbor in Provincetown, in memory of the men lost. According to James Theriault in his book *Every First Monday*, "A broken circle of metal at the base of the cross is part of the sealing ring from the *S-4* conning tower brought up in the net of a fisherman and placed with the cross."

Robert E. Lee

Rescuers Lost in Tragedy

There is still among us the stuff of which heroes are made.
Duty, after all, looms big in times of crisis.
—editorial, Chatham Monitor, *Chatham, Massachusetts, March 15, 1928*

On the night of March 9, 1928, Captain Harland W. Robinson steered the steamer *Robert E. Lee* toward Boston, along the southeastern Massachusetts coast, after passing through the Cape Cod Canal. A wild snowstorm was raging outside, with gale-force winds stirring up the seas. Looking for the beam of Gurnet Lighthouse, visibility was minimal because of the driving snow.

Twenty-two-year-old Maurice Holland, the ship's radio operator, was jolted from his seat at around 8:00 p.m. "I was in my radio office…when I heard a crash," he told the *New York Times*. "The jar was so heavy I knew something serious had happened. A minute or two later, someone poked his head in through the door and shouted, 'We have hit a rock!'"

Thanks to a heroic joint rescue effort, the passengers and crew of the *Robert E. Lee*, a 375-foot, 5,184-ton steamer, were all safely taken to shore. Three men from the Manomet Coast Guard Station wouldn't be so fortunate. The *Robert E. Lee* grounded on the treacherous Mary Ann Rocks just southeast of Manomet Point. As John J. Galluzzo noted in his article for the U.S. Life-Saving Service Preservation Association's "Wreck and Rescue," "The *Robert E. Lee* missed the first set of rocks, but struck and ran hard aground on the second. The vessel began to ship water on its starboard side, and Robinson ordered the seacocks opened, settling the *Lee*."

Robinson later blamed the compass, the *New York Times* reported. Had the *Lee* escaped the Mary Ann Rocks, and if the tide had been higher, the ship would have piled up at Indian Head, three miles farther on. "Captain Robinson attributed the changing of the compass largely to the penetration into the pilot house of large quantities of snow, driven in through the windows by the severe gale."

According to the *Times*, Holland sent a message to the Radio Corporation of America in Chatham, explaining that the ship ran aground. "I knew at that time that if the ship had not been resting on a reef, we would have all gone to the bottom," he said. Robinson, who the *Boston Globe* reported was "said to be one of the most capable of the Eastern Steamship Company's captains," then came in and ordered Holland to send an SOS call, but water was flooding the engine room, forcing Holland and his radio operator partner, John Smith, to power auxiliary batteries with a gasoline engine. By midnight, high tide was closing in, and Robinson began to fear for the vessel's safety. But, as Galluzzo noted, "the stranding had been so relatively gentle that some of the two hundred seventy-three passengers slept through the entire incident."

The *Globe* reported that second pilot Roy Litchfield referred to the passengers' morale as "one hundred percent." After the anchors were let go, Robinson had his crew mingle with the passengers to tell them they were out of danger. Others, however, were not so cooperative. The *Globe* noted that third engineer James Harvey told of how "the firemen were in stampede when the ship grounded and had to be driven back by the engineer officers." The *Times* reported that there were allegations from some passengers that, after the stranding, stewards had charged exorbitant prices for sandwiches and ginger ale.

At the Manomet Station, Boatswain's Mate William Cashman was filling in for Keeper Arthur Young, who was confined to a sickbed at his home in Orleans. Cashman and his crew tried to contact the steamer by flashing light for an hour, to no avail. At dawn, Cashman and his crew of Frank Griswold, Edward Stark, Alden Proctor, Irving Wood, Joseph Ducharme and a local mechanic named Ernest Douglas launched a surfboat and headed out for the *Lee* through the raging surf.

During the night, several rescue boats arrived at the scene, including the destroyer SS *Paulding* and the cutter *Tuscarora*, two other patrol boats. Also on hand were two motor lifeboats—one from the Sandwich station at the entrance to the Cape Cod Canal, the other from Wood End Station in Provincetown, directly across Cape Cod Bay. The Sandwich crew, led by

Chief Boatswain's Mate Anthony Tarvis, went through a search of over five hours around the bay, searching for the steamer. As the March 11, 1928 edition of the *Boston Globe* reported:

> *The* Lee*'s engine rooms were already flooded, she no longer had lights or whistle to signal her location, and if she sent up rockets they could not be seen for the snow. At 9 p.m. they were alongside, ready to begin taking off the passengers. In the first two boatloads of the old sea rule, "women first," held.*

Tarvis, who had been working at sea since the age of eleven, and his men took off seven boatloads of people. "I was never out on a worse night, and I never saw a crowd of people so cheerful and orderly," he said. "They came aboard with a smile and a 'Thank You.'" Robinson checked off names as those rescued stepped on to the lifeboat.

Out at Wood End, Captain Emanuel Gracie plodded against the gale for a mile before they could find a suitable spot to launch their lifeboat across stormy Cape Cod Bay. According to the *Cape Cod Standard-Times*, Gracie and his crew arrived shortly after midnight and transferred 115 passengers from the *Lee* to safety.

Cashman went aboard the *Lee* to discuss passenger removal, but the lifeboats had the situation under control and a surfboat shuttle would be dangerous. Just after 11:00 a.m., Cashman and his men headed back to shore. Galluzzo then described the disaster that followed:

> *A wave, described by one of the Coast Guardsmen as twenty-five feet in height, lifted the stern of the craft, jamming the bow into the seafloor, pitchpoling it onto the top of the crew. The seven stunned men floated helplessly in the water, shocked and injured from the vessel's unexpected overturning. Two hundred spectators watched on shore as Surfman Griswold momentarily surfaced, and then sank out of sight. Boatswain's Mate Cashman clung to an oar as Surfman Stark complained to his friends Proctor, Ducharme and Wood that he had severe pain around his heart. Wood, who believed that the gunwale had struck Proctor when the boat flipped, helped push him onto the overturned vessel.*

The *New York Times* described the spill in its March 11, 1928 edition:

> *They appeared to be making good headway when she was lifted clear of the water by a tremendous wave, and before it could settle down again a second*

> *wave whacked it under the bow. The craft stuck straight into the air for an instant and then flopped backward.*

Spotting the tragedy unfolding in the waves, local residents Russell Anderson, Earl Harper and Massachusetts state trooper John Horgan sprang into action, rowing in a dory to the scene. Lobstermen Harry F. Eddy and his friend Daniel Sullivan rowed another dory out. Cashman, Proctor and Wood were pulled in by Anderson's boat, while Eddy and Sullivan retrieved Stark and Ducharme. Douglas, still in the water, said, "I can hang on. Take someone else first."

Griswold, twenty-three, of Manomet, went under and never came back up; his body was recovered two days later at the foot of a cliff about a mile and a half south of the Manomet Coast Guard Station, the *Times* reported. His lifebelt, oilskins and boots were missing, and it was thought he threw them away in a desperate attempt to swim ashore after the surfboat capsized. Stark, twenty-eight, of Taunton, died on the way to Jordan Hospital in Plymouth that afternoon from exhaustion and exposure. Rescuers tried, in vain, to resuscitate Cashman on the beach for two hours before he was pronounced dead. Cashman had given up his life preserver to one of his crew members prior to their last trip to shore. As the *Times* noted:

> *A human chain was formed and a stretcher bearing the inert Cashman was passed hand over hand up the hill. His boots had fallen off in the water and his body was terribly scourged from immersion.*

The March 1928 disaster wasn't the first time that the *Lee* was involved in a collision. On December 12, 1927, the *Robert E. Lee* rammed and sank the tugboat *Neponset* off Dumpling Rock near Monquit, Buzzards Bay. Two of the tug's crew of seven drowned. The *Lee* was exonerated of blame for that accident.

Large traffic jams soon filled up the local roads. Ten thousand cars journeyed to Manomet, many from outside the state. According to the March 29, 1928 edition of the *Chatham Monitor*, water-soaked cargo from the *Lee* drifted across to Wellfleet and other towns on the Outer Cape:

> *Treasure hunters have combed the beaches all along in search of such as the sea gave up, which included a mixed assortment ranging in variety from enough face powder and other cosmetics to fix up the ladies for life on the Cape to "O'Boy" chewing gum, which latter succulent delight in large*

> *quantities has been chewed noisily by young and old. They say the salt water which they squeeze out of it doesn't hurt the flavor one bit.*

Questions lingered long after the disaster as a memorial was built to honor those lost. "In the end, the locals surmised, the Coast Guardsmen of Manomet Point had been left powerless to save their own lives," Galluzzo commented. The memorial, erected two months later at Manomet Point, reads:

> *In memory of Boatswain's Mate William H. Cashman, Surfman Frank W. Griswold, Surfman Edward P. Stark, who of Station No. 31 United States Coast Guard lost their lives in the performance of their duty, March 10, 1928, when the Steamship* Robert E. Lee *stranded on the Mary Ann Rocks Southeast of this station.*
>
> *"Greater love hath no man than this, that a man lay down his life for his friends."*

The *New York Times* concluded its March 11, 1928 coverage of the disaster by telling how a quiet group assembled at the Manomet Station following the disaster:

> *Joe Ducharme, swathed in warm clothing, murmured: "What a break. Cashman was a man among men."*
>
> *No one spoke. Silence meant agreement.*

ANNA SOPHIA

DOG DAYS OF WINTER

The husky Cape Codders put their shoulders to their rugged little craft, and over the ice she skidded, and into the calmest spot in many miles.
—Boston Globe, *February 10, 1934*

During recent winters on Cape Cod, television and internet outlets went heavy on coverage of waves of slush that were washing ashore on Cape Cod's Outer Beach. Then, of course, there's the regular dose of dog stories and social media posts on any given day. So put those two together, and one can only imagine what the media feeding frenzy would have been (and deservedly so) over the Coast Guard's glacial rescue of the crew from two-masted schooner *Anna Sophia* off Eastham's Nauset Spit on February 9, 1934, which involved Cape Codders, Coast Guardsmen, captains and canines.

Keeper George Nickerson and the crew of the Nauset Coast Guard Station pulled off the heroic rescue of the five-man crew and its poodle mascot, "Spud," in subzero temperatures from the distressed 102-foot vessel bound for Lubec, Maine, from New York. After finding an opening through a wall of ice (which ranged anywhere in size from two to ten feet, depending on which account you believe) that had built up along the shoreline, the crew and its tractor were forced to pull their surfboat nearly two hundred yards down the beach before a suitable opening for a launch could be found. "A small patch of beach, on either side of which breakers rolled in, yielded the most suited spot," according to the February 10, 1934 edition of the *Boston Globe*.

Fearing that their anchored two-masted schooner might be shredded to pieces after a blizzard, the crew of the *Anna Sophia* took to a dory. *Cape Cod National Seashore.*

The *Anna Sophia* had its sails ripped to shreds during a blizzard the night before and, after spotting the beacon of Nauset Light, anchored about one mile off Eastham. Captain John Peabody feared that the vessel might be shattered to pieces, and the crew was lowered into the dory in a high-risk escape attempt to shore.

"Captain Nickerson instructed two of us to chop a clearing in the ice rather than try to push the boat over it," Joseph Berbine, one of the six crew members, told Mike Maynard of the Coast Guard Heritage Museum in Barnstable. "The tide was high…the seas that day were choppy. I recall that a sort of slush ice was on the surface near the shore, keeping the seas from breaking on the beach. It took us about an hour to row out to the schooner."

With the passing of the storm, the wind had shifted to the west-northwest, sweeping the dory back out to sea. The surfboat reached it a mile to a mile and a half out at sea, and two boathooks held the dory close as the crew was transferred. Nickerson was able to find the same opening in the ice on the return to the beach. Crew members and Coast Guardsmen alike were rushed back to the station for frostbite treatment. The Coast Guard rescue effort included Nickerson, Berbine, Yngve Rongner, Ralph Ormsby,

The crew of the *Anna Sophia*, along with their poodle, Spud, following their rescue from the frigid Atlantic off Eastham in February 1934. *Cape Cod National Seashore.*

The crew of the Nauset Coast Guard Station had to drag their surfboat two hundred yards down the beach to find an opening in a wall of ice to rescue the *Anna Sophia* crew. *Cape Cod National Seashore.*

The Coast Guard cutter *Dix* later towed the *Anna Sophia* to Provincetown, where it was repaired. The vessel later completed its journey to Maine. *Cape Cod National Seashore.*

Jules Serpa, James Brown and Henry Hautenan. Spud fared better than his human counterparts. As the *Globe* reported:

> *When the surfboat and her load of hardy Maine fishermen rode through the breakers to an ice caked shore, "Spud," got a shower of surf, but dashed out of the arms which held to greet the Coast Guard station's mascot, Rex, a big police dog, which awaited the return of his masters.*

On February 11, the Coast Guard cutter *Dix* reached the *Anna Sophia* and towed it to Provincetown. A photograph revealed a twisted and ice-covered sail and rigging, with eight inches of water covering the deck. The vessel was fitted with new sails, and the crew would complete the journey to Maine. As the *Globe* put it, "The rescue of the crew of the *Anna Sophia* will go down as another heroic page in Coast Guard annals." That's a fact that neither man nor dog would dispute.

Lutzen

Blueberries on the Beach

Everyone in Eastham, Orleans and the Lower Cape had more blueberries than they knew what to do with. We had blueberry pie, blueberry muffins, blueberries and sugar, blueberries and cream…you name it. The only problem was that the salt water had gotten into the ship, so if you liked salted blueberries, they were delicious.
—Fenton Sparrow, as told to the Eastham Historical Society

Whenever ships stranded on Cape Cod's outer bar, it was common practice for some locals, often referred to as "wreckers," to salvage whatever cargo might be in the vessel's hold. Usually, it was something along the lines of wood laths, sugar, coffee, alcoholic beverages or even salt or granite. However, it was a different prize for the locals when the *Lutzen*, a 339-ton British freighter, struck the foggy sandbars of Nauset Beach in Orleans on February 2, 1939—it was blueberries for everyone.

En route from Nova Scotia to New York, the *Lutzen* was carrying one hundred barrels of cod liver oil, some frozen cod and 250 tons of frozen blueberries, but fog and rough seas made for a treacherous trip. After nearly a week at sea, Captain Robert Randall and his crew skirted the coast of Cape Cod, thinking that they were near the *Pollock* lightship. Due to poor visibility, they were actually a mere seventy-five yards offshore when the *Lutzen* struck the sandbar between the Orleans and Old Harbor Coast Guard Stations.

Coast Guardsman Ed Dorion of the Old Harbor Station was heading north on his patrol, spotted the *Lutzen* and fired a flare just as the vessel was

The freighter *Lutzen*, carrying a load of frozen blueberries, stranded along Nauset Beach in Orleans on February 2, 1939. *Sturgis Library Archives.*

hitting the sand. Randall then ordered two of his men to board a lifeboat and head for shore, hoping to find out who fired the warning flare and to seek help. However, the surf proved to be too much, overturning the boat and claiming the life of twenty-eight-year-old Baxter Bailey. The other man was able to grab a line and was pulled from the raging surf. During the night, Coast Guardsmen from the Orleans and Old Harbor Stations were able to rescue the remaining eight crew members with a breeches buoy.

In an attempt to lighten the *Lutzen*'s load, one hundred barrels of cod liver oil were broken open and thrown overboard. According to the February 10, 1939 edition of the *Yarmouth Register*, "frozen blueberries from St. Johns, New Brunswick, which largely made up the cargo, were spoiled when the ship's refrigeration motors stopped." It was a race against the clock—"the wave action was just beating it apart," Fenton Sparrow told the Eastham Historical Society. Four days later, the *Lutzen* rolled over on its beam ends and was a total loss.

However, some of the freely available fruit was salvageable, and many locals helped themselves. As Jim Coogan wrote in the June 24, 2011 edition of the *Barnstable Patriot*, "Many of the Coast Guardsmen were related to the scavengers and looked the other way as boxes of fruit disappeared."

Reta (Cummings) Sparrow was one of those locals, recovering several crates of berries. Her husband, Don Sparrow, told the Eastham Historical Society:

> [She] *realized that to carry these crates off the beach, it was a long, long walk, and then Bud Fisher then came by with a truck. He helped her get them back in exchange for blueberry pies. He was working at a restaurant in the summer and living off unemployment in the winter. He'd come from off Cape and he and his friends would feast on blueberry pies that Rita was making for them.*

For most Cape Codders, though, as Coogan put it, "After four or five weeks, the steady offerings of the salvaged fruit grew pretty tiresome." The *Lutzen* ended up making another type of delivery to the Outer Cape, resulting in a boost to the area's rodent population. The February 9, 1939 edition of the *Provincetown Advocate* reported, "Several rats, living in the hold of the *Lutzen*, came on deck when the boat capsized and made their way ashore across the hawsers attached to the boat."

Cape Ann

Icy Spectacle in Eastham

In contrast to the high cliff, rugged beach, and wide expanse of ocean, the ice-coated ship appeared as a broken toy of the elements to the spectators.
—Arthur G. Dickey, Cape Codder, *March 11, 1948*

By the 1940s, ship disasters were on the decline along Cape Cod's Outer Beach. The Cape Cod Canal had become the preferred route for mariners, but the occasional wreck still occurred, such as the New Bedford–based scalloper *Cape Ann*'s demise just north of Nauset Light at 3:00 a.m. on March 6, 1948.

The eighty-two-foot vessel, carrying a load of scallops valued between $4,000 and $5,000, was returning from a ten-day fishing trip on George's Bank. The temperature was hovering just above zero, and winds were approaching gale force when the first mate mistook Nauset Light for the *Pollock* lightship.

The Coast Guard's rescue attempts with amphibious ducks came up empty, so the breeches buoy was utilized for the first time in many years. Five of the nine crew members were pulled in by way of the primitive zip line, while four others remained on board with the cargo and played cards while waiting. They even managed a meal. The *New York Times* reported that "a hardy cook stood waist deep in water to cook bacon and eggs."

The wreck on the Eastham beach wasn't the first for *Cape Ann*'s Captain Axel Nerland of New Bedford—he wrecked three times before on this beach, according to the March 7, 1948 edition of the *Boston Globe*. It was also another adventurous chapter in the life of Patrick Kelley of Staten Island, New York, who was previously in the navy for eight years. Kelley was on four carriers that were torpedoed in the Pacific during World War II: the *Wasp*, *Hornet*, *Franklin* and *Hamilton*. He was taken prisoner by the Japanese to Luzon and was rescued by marines.

When the tide subsided after sunrise, the remaining men on board were able to walk ashore. The Coast Guard "was reinforced in rescue operations by courageous civilians," according to the March 11, 1948 edition of the *Cape Codder*.

Coast Guardsmen and civilians who maintained a vigil before daylight Saturday until night were provided food by Eastham residents and members of Nauset Ship, Sea Scouts, of Orleans. One family made and delivered ten gallons of beef stew to rescue workers. According to the *Cape Codder*, the Sea Scouts were led by Dr. R. Frederick Raddin, skipper, and David Delano and Norman White, mates. They were offered one of the two spars of the ship in appreciation by the ship's owner, Leon Dobson of New Bedford. The Scouts arrived at the beach at 8:00 a.m. and had pots of coffee and soup boiling over driftwood fires on the beach. Crew members from the *Cape Ann* were reluctant to eat the food, as their money

The New Bedford scalloper *Cape Ann* stranded just north of Nauset Light in Eastham on a frigid night in March 1948. Local residents provided the crew members with hot food. *Mary McDermott.*

was still aboard the vessel. "No payment was expected or wanted," and "the seamen ate heartily," the *Cape Codder* reported.

Word of the wreck spread quickly, and "throngs of weekenders and Cape residents visited the scene," according to the *Cape Codder*. Many ventured down the sixty-five-foot cliff to the beach, while others observed from high on the cliff. Cars lined the roads near the lighthouse. "The wreck…had all of the elements of suspense," the *Cape Codder* noted. "Metropolitan newspapers and radio newscasters were quick to seize upon its drama."

By 1948, the Coast Guard beach patrols had ceased. Abbott Walker, who was the keeper at the nearby Nauset Station from 1905 to 1926, told the *Cape Codder* shortly after the *Cape Ann* wreck that this was not a wise move on the part of his former employer. "They never ought to have taken the patrol off," Walker said. "If that last wreck had been out of sight of the Coast Guard station, all those men might have been lost."

Evgenia

Aground on the Outer Bar

[The *Evgenia*] *became the cause of rich pay-dirt for beach buggy operators.*
—Provincetown Advocate, *September 17, 1953*

On the morning of September 7, 1953, shortly after 5:00 a.m., Captain Elias Sharellis and the crew of the Greek freighter *Evgenia* were doing everything possible to stay out of the path of Hurricane Carol, a monster tropical system that was passing 140 miles east of Cape Cod and heading for Nova Scotia.

Only a day earlier, the storm was rated as a Category 5 hurricane, but it began to lose some strength as it pushed farther north. The 225-foot, 3,500-ton vessel, which was heading from Baltimore to Saint John, Nova Scotia, proved to be no match for the turbulent seas and was soon stuck in the sand one mile east of the Peaked Hill Bar Coast Guard Station in Provincetown.

The ship would remain stuck in the sand for five days, with most of the seventeen crew members rescued by breeches buoy, the next-to-last time that this piece of apparatus would be utilized on Cape Cod. The remaining men were rescued by the Nauset Station's DUKW (an amphibious vehicle also known as a "Duck"). The spectacle also drew thousands of curious onlookers to the back shore of Provincetown.

The September 10, 1953 edition of the *Provincetown Advocate* quoted Michael Moskouris, the ship's cook, as saying that the *Evgenia* heeded the hurricane warning and hugged the coastline when "the trouble began." The *Advocate* reported that "her crew said she was being tossed around like a

Seventeen crew members from the freighter *Evgenia* were rescued by breeches buoy. It was the next-to-last time that that this piece of apparatus was used on Cape Cod. *Cape Cod National Seashore.*

floating bottle, attributing her 'uncontrollable' actions to the lack of freight and a broken propeller." Shortly after striking the bar, Captain Sharellis radioed in a message to the Coast Guard: "Am aground near Cape Cod Lighthouse. Position unsafe on account of coming hurricane. Please keep contact with us in case of emergency." One hour later, Coast Guard units from around Cape Cod were responding. Chief Boatswain's Mate Everett M. Marshall, in charge of all lifeboat stations along the Cape, ordered crews to search the shorelines.

Coast Guardsmen from all Outer Cape stations from Chatham to Race Point took part in the rescue, according to the September 8, 1953 edition of the *Cape Cod Standard-Times*. A special field telephone was installed by the Chatham telephone unit, headed by Raymond W. Nickerson, electricians mate first class. A surfboat rescue attempt was made later that morning, but the rough seas forced the Coast Guard to abort the mission. At this point, the old breeches buoy was brought out of retirement, with Moskouris, one of the few *Evgenia* crew members who could speak English, getting the first lift ashore at 11:00 a.m. Each breeches buoy session took more than twenty minutes. The thirteenth man, forty-three-year-old seaman Steve Evagelis, fell five feet into the water when the line snapped. He was pulled from the water by local resident Thomas Comes, Robert Panico of Boston and Alfred Fearing of Winthrop. Panico and Fearing were staying at a Provincetown campground and were among the visitors to the beach. The initial twelve men rescued were taken to the Nauset Station. Evagelis recovered from his shock and soon joined them for a bus ride to Boston. Captain Sharellis and a handful of crew members stayed aboard to assist in salvage operations.

By the following weekend, the tugboat *Curb* was at the scene. Despite the significant difference in size between the two vessels, the *Evgenia* was soon headed to Boston, according to the September 17, 1953 edition of the *Provincetown Advocate*:

> *Amazement, admiration and relief mingled as Cape End folks and their visitors watched the appearance around Long Point Saturday afternoon of the Greek freighter, Panama registered,* Evgenia, *the ship that was doomed, that would never be moved from Peaked Hill bars where she struck early on Monday of last week, and from which she was removed shortly after noon Saturday. The* Curb*…had that air of cocksure determination, common to tugs, and wasn't taking any nonsense from the big hulk she had pulled practically from dry land.*

Monica Smith

Smorgasbord on the Sand

Thousands of cars streamed to the State Beach at Provincetown, parked and their occupants walked the mile or so down the beach to scratch initials on the ship's plates.
—Cape Codder, *February 1960*

During the early winter months of 1960, the St. Mary of the Harbor Church in Provincetown planned a smorgasbord supper for Saturday night, February 20. Little did the Episcopal congregation—or anyone else on the Cape tip—realize just how big of a Swedish supper event that winter weekend would turn out to be. It was on this night the 258-foot Swedish freighter *Monica Smith* ran aground at Hatches Harbor, just south of Race Point, during a "clear-skied gale," according to the *Cape Codder*. It would take several attempts and six days before the vessel was able to resume its run from New Bedford to Nova Scotia.

"When the tide went out, she was completely out of water and made a perfect attraction for Cape residents on the holiday weekend," the *Cape Codder* reported. As one veteran policeman noted, "It looks like the middle of July," and you don't have to be a Wall Street executive to know that means the cash registers were ringing. As the *Cape Codder* noted:

> *The event was an unexpected boon to Cape-end business. Those Provincetown restaurants that were open soon ran out of food. And you couldn't buy a roll of film until you got back to Orleans. Camera enthusiasts had a field day and good photographs were a dime a dozen.*

The 258-foot Swedish freighter *Monica Smith* ran aground at Hatches Harbor, just south of Race Point in Provincetown, on February 20, 1960. *Sturgis Library Archives.*

Another local newspaper had this account:

> *Not since the total eclipse of the sun back in '32 have we seen such an off-season run of traffic to the Cape. We've heard reports that roadside petrol stations are doing summer business volume, and more than one Truro man has been heard to murmur he wished had a quarter for every car that's rolled down the pike since the freighter* Monica Smith *went ashore near Race Point in Provincetown. Chief Berrio says he has been on the highway constantly, patrolling the stream of automobiles.*

As for the Stockholm-based freighter, it had already unloaded 2,500 tons of cement at Fall River and dropped off 150 small cars in Halifax, Nova Scotia. On board, there was still 20 tons of Danish blue cheese, along with the *Monica Smith*'s disgruntled captain, John Gustrind. Reasons for the mishap "remained obscure as her master sulked in his cabin, refusing to discuss matters," the *Cape Codder* reported.

On Monday, February 23, tugs moved the grounded vessel a few feet before a cable snapped. Three days later, Captain Frank A. Shepherd—salvage master for Merritt, Chapman and Scott Salvage Company—was finally successful. The vessel was set free by the tugboat *Orion*.

It would take several attempts over six days before the *Monica Smith* was able to resume its run from New Bedford to Nova Scotia. *Phil Cole.*

The stranding of the freighter *Monica Smith* led to a big boon for business during the winter, as many people flocked to Provincetown to see the spectacle. *Phil Cole.*

The *Monica Smith* was freed early on February 25, reached Provincetown Harbor shortly after noon and then left at 5:30 p.m. to complete the trip to Saint John, New Brunswick, after getting approval from inspectors. The vessel gave a farewell burst of its whistle upon leaving the harbor and, according to the February 26, 1960 edition of the *Cape Cod Standard Times*, gave "Long Point a wide berth as she led to resume her interrupted voyage." The paper had a photograph of twelve-year-old Tucker Souza, son of Chief Boatswain's Mate Arthur Souza of the Race Point Coast Guard Station, bidding the *Monica Smith* farewell.

With local eateries running low on food, the *Cape Codder* reported that some locals "suggested that it might be a good idea to open a Swedish restaurant on board." Local electrician Al Bettencourt happened to overhear Wellfleet's Henry Carlson acting as a translator for the Scandinavian ship's crew as they were hoisting boxes of groceries on board. "I noticed a big bag of linguica in the grocery box," Bettencourt said. "Wonder how Henry explained what that was in Swedish?"

MARGARET ROSE

BREECHES BUOY'S SWAN SONG

We brought seven men ashore in those [breeches] *buoys. I had never handled them, not once. Bernie* [Webber] *told us what to do—he was good in situations like that.*
—Ben Davidson, as told to the Cape Codder, *2009*

The breeches buoy was one of the great tools of the trade for the men of the U.S. Life-Saving Service and the U.S. Coast Guard during the late nineteenth century and first half of the twentieth century, but by 1962, it had become a historic relic. On January 16, 1962, the breeches buoy was used for the very last time on a Cape Cod beach, during the rescue of the seven-man crew from the Gloucester fishing vessel *Margaret Rose*, carrying five tons of halibut, off Wood End Light in Provincetown.

Just before 4:00 a.m., *Margaret Rose*'s Captain Peter Petrosino lost his electrical navigation gear while working his way through sixty-mile-per-hour southeasterly gales, according to the January 18, 1962 edition of the *Cape Codder*. A helicopter arrived from the Salem Air Station and amphibious DUKWs from the Race Point and Chatham Stations were at the scene, but it was clear to Chief Boatswain's Mate Bernie Webber that this was going to be more of an old-school rescue attempt.

Webber, best known for his heroic efforts in the *Pendleton* rescue a decade earlier, had "been fighting an uphill battle to keep the breeches buoy from being phased out and the nearest equipment was at the Cape Cod Canal station in Sandwich," reported the April 10, 1984 edition of the

Cape Codder. It wasn't long before the breeches buoy was hauled out to the Provincetown beach. "Gathering a bunch of green men, and designating them positions, we rigged the breeches buoy to the Margaret Rose, and removed seven men in this way," Webber later wrote. "As luck would have it, our first shot was successful."

"Her hull was facing the beach and her masts were facing the ocean, and there were thirty-five-foot waves coming in," Ben Davidson, Webber's friend and fellow Coast Guard member, told the *Cape Codder* in 2009. "There was no way to take the boat around to seaward without going in yourself."

Webber and his young crew went to work. According to the January 18, 1962 edition of the *Provincetown Advocate*, "Coast Guard Seaman Vincent Thompson of the Race Point Station plunged from the shore into the angry white surf, carrying a line attached to a cable for a distance of seventy-five to one hundred yards out to the vessel, in preparation for attaching the breeches buoy."

Joseph Passanisi of Somerville was the first fisherman rescued. He had attempted to swing himself along the cable, hand over hand, but slipped off into the surf. Coast Guardsmen assisting him were Davidson, seaman Roger Davis and engineman William Wolf of the Race Point Station. Fisherman Nicolo Sanfilipo of Everett also lost his hold on the cable and fell in. The waves tossed him back on deck, causing cuts and bruises.

Eventually, everyone was hauled ashore by the breeches buoy, which was then sent off into retirement. Twenty-four years later, it was nearly called into service once again.

ELDIA

SHOWCASE ON THE SHORE

Neither Congressmen nor bureaucrats are called upon to hover over thirty-foot seas in a mid-winter storm at midnight risking their lives to save others. As a country, we ask much of the Coast Guard and in doing so we incur obligation of our own.
—U.S. Congressman Gerry Studds of Massachusetts, quoted by the Cape Codder *of Orleans, Massachusetts, April 10, 1984*

During the late afternoon hours of March 29, 1984, lobsterman Michael Kartasiewicz was in his home along the Nauset Heights section of Orleans when he heard commotion stirring in the stormy conditions that had intensified about an hour earlier. Out the door he ran, spotting a large freighter in distress out at sea.

"She was just foundering," Kartasiewicz told the *Cape Codder* newspaper for its April 3, 1984 edition. "She was broadside to the sea. Waves were crashing over the bow. I saw her hit the outer bar. She hit hard and started listing at about forty-five degrees. I thought she was going to lay right over. She was flat bottom. I thought she would break up."

The vessel was the *Eldia*, a 471-foot freighter heading from New Brunswick, Nova Scotia, to Norfolk, Virginia. Thanks to the heroic efforts of the Coast Guard, the crew of the ship, which was owned by Thenmaris Inc. of Athens, Greece, and registered in Bolleta, Malta, all survived, but the stranding led to a spectacle that brought thousands of off-season visitors to Nauset Beach. "Traffic was as heavy, or probably heavier, than a hot August day," said Orleans police chief Donald Walsh.

A rescue helicopter passes over the *Eldia* on Nauset Beach in Orleans following the freighter's stranding in March 1984. *From the* Cape Codder, *Orleans, Massachusetts.*

Orleans historian William Quinn, who authored the booklet *The Grounding of the Eldia on Nauset Beach…a Pictorial Event*, noted that the site of the stranding was within one hundred feet of where the *Sparrow-Hawk* wrecked in 1626. It would sit on the shore for forty-eight days, with the project costing hundreds of thousands of dollars.

According to an extensive 2019 exhibit curated by the Orleans Historical Society, the *Eldia* "remained upright, struck parallel to the shore, and was in imminent danger of breaking up." First Mate Manuel Villagracia admitted to the *Cape Codder* that "we couldn't control" the *Eldia* after the storm intensified. Four miles north of Nauset Beach, Captain Ernesto Garces tried to swing the vessel around and head back to Cape Cod Bay. "She just kept turning in circles, turning in circles," Villagracia said.

After hitting the bar, the *Eldia* was pushed right up to the beach. "It was quite a scene," Kartasiewicz marveled. "It was spectacular." Quinn added that "the vessel was light in the water and high seas caused her to pitch and yaw out of control." The force of the ship's impact on the beach threw the crewmen to the floor.

According to the Orleans Historical Society, an H-3 twin-turbine Coast Guard rescue helicopter was dispatched from Otis Air Force Base, and a crew from Coast Guard station Chatham, under the direction of Chief Tom Pezzi, reported to the scene. Police and fire personnel from Orleans, Eastham, Chatham, Harwich and Brewster were called out, with Hyannis,

Yarmouth and Wellfleet crews standing by. As a backup, breeches buoy apparatus from the Orleans Historical Society, not used in more than twenty years, was brought to the beach but was not needed.

With little time to waste, a helicopter airlift rescue commenced at 5:07 p.m. As night set in, "We had to get the crew off before dark," Orleans fire chief Raphael Merrill told the *Cape Codder*. "If the chopper couldn't get them and they had to abandon ship, we never would have found them in the water. We would have had some casualties there."

The *Cape Codder* reported that the helicopter made three attempts using a basket, taking eight, thirteen and two crew hands, respectively. The helicopter was also running out of fuel. The *Cape Codder* noted that if they hadn't gotten the thirteen off during the second run, they never would have gotten them all off.

Sixty-mile-per-hour winds made the helicopter flight difficult, especially when taking off and dropping off the crewmen in the Nauset Beach parking lot. The helicopter crew consisted of pilot Lieutenant David Cooper, copilot Jim McManus, flight mechanic Jeff Amatrudo and radio operator Chuck Hancock.

Coast Guard spokesman Lieutenant Eric Shaw called the rescue one of the finest he ever saw. "There's a basic tenet in the maritime world: 'A grounding can ruin your entire day,'" he told the *Cape Codder*. The paper reported that the *Eldia* crewmen were fed coffee, soup and sandwiches at the Orleans Fire Station and then stayed at the Cove Motel and were served breakfast at Ardath's the next day.

While lives were quickly saved, a potential ecological disaster was in the making. The Orleans Historical Society noted that Clean Harbor Inc. pumped 140,000 gallons of fuel oil from the ship, using three thousand feet of rubber hose across the beach, connected to trucks for transport to New Bedford. Donjon Marine and McAllister Towing and Salvage were engaged to re-float the *Eldia*. Twenty-three holes in the hold had to be patched with steel plates and quickset concrete. The damaged hull also had to be reinforced with steel I-beams. Fortunately, only 100 gallons of leaked fuel had to be mitigated.

Quinn noted that after the storm ended, "The ship lay stranded on the sands like a big whale. A sandbar was building up around her gently deposited by each tide." The *Century*, an offshore salvage derrick, arrived at Nauset Beach from New York by tug and was connected to the *Eldia* by cables. Taking advantage of lunar high tides, the ship was turned at night. The blocks were reset the next day and the process repeated. On May 17, the *Eldia* was finally re-floated and towed through the Cape Cod Canal to Newport, Rhode Island, for evaluation.

While the ordeal could have been much worse, the stranding also translated into big business for Cape Cod merchants. Quinn noted that "on Cape Cod, word of a ship in trouble spreads like wildfire. In no time at all, there were a hundred people on the beach." Shelby Scott of WBZ-TV in Boston reported that during "the first weekend, an estimated 30,000 people trekked across the dunes to see [the *Eldia*]."

The town of Orleans began to charge two dollars for beach parking. Local entrepreneurs produced souvenir mugs and T-shirts. Eastham's Noel Beyle sold more than twenty thousand postcards. Joan Hart of Quahog Hollow in Orleans told WBZ-TV that she sold "well over 3,000" *Eldia* coffee mugs.

Even the local restaurants prospered. Donna Smith of the East Orleans Deli told WBZ-TV that they "had a 'Shipwreck Sandwich,' with turkey, cranberry sauce, and cheese in a pocket rolled up." John Murphy of the Land Ho! in Orleans told the *Cape Codder* that business was better than on a rainy Saturday in July. Those who ordered clam chowder found a plastic freighter floating atop the potatoes. "I think everyone benefitted from it," he said, "except the fellow who owns the ship."

Bibliography

Newspapers

Barnstable Patriot. January 12, 1895; April 5, 1912; April 25, 1916; February 13, 1922; January 1, 1923; October 16, 1924; June 24, 2011.

Boston Globe. September 15, 1896; December 29, 1896; August 21, 1904; September 4, 1904; February 18, 1914; February 15, 1922; March 6, 1927; March 21, 1927; March 10–16, 1928; March 7, 1948.

Boston Herald. October, 1898.

Boston Post. September 15, 1896; October 15, 1913; March 27, 1925.

Cape Cod Standard-Times/Cape Cod Times. September 8, 1953; February 26, 1960; May 5, 1963; September 10, 1968; October 17, 1968; August 17, 1980.

Cape Codder. March 11, 1948; July 29, 1948; November 18, 1948; April 9, 1950; March 3, 1960; April 3, 1981; April 3, 1984; April 10, 1984; May 8, 2009.

Chatham Monitor. December 7, 1880; February 2, 1897; March 15, 1928; January 14, 1937.

Hyannis Patriot. January 26, 1907; December 25, 1930.

New Bedford Evening Standard. February 21, 1927.

New York Herald. February 1911.

New York Times. February 8, 1922; February 9, 1922; March 10–16, 1928.

Provincetown Advocate. January 1, 1873; March 11, 1875; January 10, 1878; December 22, 1928; February 9, 1939; July 30, 1942; May 9, 1946; August

12, 1948; December 2, 1948; March 3, 1949; March 10, 1949; March 31, 1949; September 10, 1953; September 17, 1953; January 18, 1962.
Yarmouth Register. April 19, 1879; September 18, 1886; January 26, 1895; February 22, 1902; January 26, 1907; June 26, 1909; March 31, 1925; November 23, 1926; December 22, 1928; September 10, 1943.

Magazines and Periodicals

Arts and Archaeology Magazine 13 (January–June 1922). The Archaeological Society of Washington.
Ballou's Pictorial Magazine (1856).
Cape Cod Way (1955).
Galluzzo, John J. *Wreck and Rescue* 5, no. 4. U.S. Life-Saving Service Preservation Association.
Harper's Monthly Magazine (1907).
Maynard, Mike. Coast Guard Heritage Museum (Barnstable, Massachusetts) newsletter, 2012.
World's Work Magazine (November 1923).

Reports

Cape Cod National Seashore. "Historic Furnishings Report: Old Harbor Lifesaving Station." 2005.
Nauset Lifesaving Station Report, 1888.
Petersen, Ron. "The Lifesaving Legacy of Orleans." Orleans Historical Society.
U.S. Life-Saving Service, Annual Reports, 1872–1915.

Books

Beston, Henry. *The Outermost House*. New York: Doubleday and Doran, 1928.
Dalton, J.W. *The Life-Savers of Cape Cod*. Boston: Barta Press, 1902.
Emery, Edwin. *The History of Sanford, Maine*. Fall River, MA: The Compiler, 1901.
Forbes, Allan, and Ralph M. Eastman. *Town and City Seals of Massachusetts.* Vol. 2. Boston: State Street Bank, 1951.

Kittredge, Henry. *Mooncussers of Cape Cod.* Boston: Houghton-Mifflin, 1937.
Noble, Dennis L. *That Others Might Live.* Annapolis, MD: Naval Institute Press, 1994.
O'Connor, William D. *Heroes of the Storm.* Boston: Houghton-Mifflin, 1904.
Perley, Sidney. *Historic Storms of New England.* Salem, MA: Salem Press and Printing Company, 1891.
Rich, Earle. *Cape Cod Echoes.* Wellfleet, MA: Earle Rich Memorial Scholarships Inc., 1973.
Shanks, Ralph C. *The U.S. Life-Saving Service: Heroes, Rescues and Architecture of the Early Coast Guard.* Novata, CA: Costaño Books, 1996.
Small, Isaac M. *Shipwrecks of Cape Cod.* Riverside, CT: Chatham Press, 1928.
Snow, Edward Rowe. *A Pilgrim Returns to Cape Cod.* Boston: Yankee Publishing Company, 1946.
Tarbell, Arthur Wilson. *Cape Cod Ahoy!* Boston: Little, Brown and Company, 1932.
Theriault, James. *Every First Monday: A History of King Hiram's Lodge, Provincetown, and Its Members, 1795–1995.* Provincetown, MA: King Hiram's Lodge, 1995.
Thoreau, Henry David. *Cape Cod.* New York: W.W. Norton and Company, 1951. Originally published in 1865.

Booklets and Pamphlets

Grozier, E.A. *The Wreck of the Somerset.* Provincetown History Project, 1886.
Quinn, William. *The Grounding of the Eldia on Nauset Beach…a Pictorial Event.* Orleans, MA: Lower Cape Publishing, 1984. Out of print but available through used book dealers and more.

Interviews

Boonisar, Richard. Interview by Don Wilding, October 2015.
Collins, Bernard. *Tales of Cape Cod.* Barnstable, MA, 1977.
Hobbs, David. Interview by Don Wilding, June 2016.
Martin, William. Interview by Don Wilding, November 2014.
Rongner, Yngve. Eastham Historical Society, undated.
Scott, Shelby. "Reports from Orleans." WBZ-TV, Boston, April 1984–85.
Snow, Bonnie. Interview by Don Wilding, June 2016.
Sparrow, Fenton. Eastham Historical Society, 1981.

Exhibits, Presentations and Blogs

Cape Cod National Seashore. "The Lifesaving Service of Cape Cod." Admiral Donald B. McMillan, 1965.

Orleans Historical Society. "Shipwrecks," 2019.

Thoreau Society. "At the Threshold of Chaos: Henry Thoreau on Cape Cod." Elizabeth Kalman, with Nicholas Holdgate.

Index

A

B

F

G

H

I

J

K

L

M

N

O

P

Q

R

S

T

U

V

W

Y

About the Author

Since the start of the millennium, Don Wilding has been telling stories of Cape Cod Outer Beach history. An award-winning writer and editor for Massachusetts newspapers since 1985, Don has contributed the "Shore Lore" history column for the *Cape Codder* newspaper of Orleans and is the author of two other books, *Henry Beston's Cape Cod: How the Outermost House Inspired a National Seashore* and *A Brief of History of Eastham: On the Outer Beach of Cape Cod*. He is also a tour guide and lecturer and has taught local history classes for adults on the Outer Cape. Don and his wife, Nita, are longtime Cape Cod residents.

dwCapeCod.com
donwildingscapecod@gmail.com